trauma-sensitive
leadership

creating a safe and predictable
school environment

JOHN F. ELLER & TOM HIERCK

Solution Tree | Press
a division of
Solution Tree

555 North Morton Street
Bloomington, IN 47404
800.733.6786 (toll free) / 812.336.7700
FAX: 812.336.7790

email: info@SolutionTree.com
SolutionTree.com

Visit **go.SolutionTree.com/leadership** to download the free reproducibles in this book.

Printed in the United States of America

Names: Eller, John, 1957- author. | Hierck, Tom, 1960- author.
Title: Trauma-sensitive leadership : creating a safe and predictable school environment / John F. Eller, Tom Hierck.
Description: Bloomington : Solution Tree Press, [2022] | Includes bibliographical references and index.
Identifiers: LCCN 2022000148 (print) | LCCN 2022000149 (ebook) | ISBN 9781949539974 (Paperback) | ISBN 9781949539981 (eBook)
Subjects: LCSH: Children with mental disabilities--Education. | Psychic trauma in children. | Post-traumatic stress disorder in children. | Educational psychology. | School environment.
Classification: LCC LC4601 E55 2022 (print) | LCC LC4601 (ebook) | DDC 371.92--dc23/eng/20220223
LC record available at https://lccn.loc.gov/2022000148
LC ebook record available at https://lccn.loc.gov/2022000149

Solution Tree
Jeffrey C. Jones, CEO
Edmund M. Ackerman, President

Solution Tree Press
President and Publisher: Douglas M. Rife
Associate Publisher: Sarah Payne-Mills
Managing Production Editor: Kendra Slayton
Editorial Director: Todd Brakke
Art Director: Rian Anderson
Copy Chief: Jessi Finn
Senior Production Editor: Christine Hood
Content Development Specialist: Amy Rubenstein
Acquisitions Editor: Sarah Jubar
Proofreader: Sarah Ludwig
Editorial Assistants: Charlotte Jones, Sarah Ludwig, and Elijah Oates

Dedication

To my wife, Sheila, who believed in me and encouraged me to lead others all those years ago. Thank you for your support. You exemplify caring for your staff and students every day. You change lives for the positive.

—John F. Eller

This book is dedicated to Travis Rosenstand, whose flame went out way too early but whose spark will continue to light the fire in the lives he touched. There are students who come into the life of an educator as a test of his or her capacity to be an educator. Travis was one of those kids who tested every ounce of patience I had as a beginning school leader, but he always had that spark you knew would carry him beyond the current moment. I sit here with tears in my eyes as I reflect on the awesome young man he became and the positive impact he had on so many, including my family. It's a reminder that life is played going forward, and a kid who struggles just needs an adult who cares. Travis, you repaid that investment and so much more. You won't be forgotten.

—Tom Hierck

Acknowledgments

Although only two names appear on the cover, this book would not be possible without the support and input of many colleagues and friends.

Beginning with our Solution Tree family, we would like to thank the following key supporters: Jeff Jones, who built a company that encourages educators to find their voice and share with colleagues; Douglas Rife, the president and publisher of Solution Tree Press, who provided us with the opportunity and encouragement to develop and write the book; Christine Hood, our senior editor, who helped refine the rough manuscript into a book that flows and makes sense for busy teachers; Sarah Ludwig, our proofreader; and Shik Love and Kelly Rockhill, whose skills in marketing and promotion will ensure this book reaches a wide audience and can have the maximum benefit to colleagues.

Solution Tree Press would like to thank the following reviewers:

Tara Fulton
Principal
Clute Intermediate
Clute, Texas

Brian Greeney
Assistant Superintendent of Innovation,
 Teaching, and Learning
Willis ISD
Willis, Texas

Larry Hausner
CEO/Founder
Coaching School Leadership
Huntington Beach, California

Ian Landy
Principal
Powell River School District
Powell River, British Columbia

Bryn M. Williams
Principal
Coquitlam School District
Coquitlam, British Columbia

Visit **go.SolutionTree.com/leadership** to download the free reproducibles in this book.

Table of Contents

About the Authors

John F. Eller, PhD, is a former principal, director of a principals' training center, and assistant superintendent for curriculum, learning, and staff development.

John is also a much sought-after consultant to schools and school districts both nationally and internationally. He specializes in trauma-sensitive teaching and leadership, school turnaround, dealing with difficult people, building collaborative teams, conducting employee evaluations, building conferencing and coaching skills, developing strategic planning strategies, building supervisory skills, and implementing effective teaching strategies. John also serves as a consultant for U.S. federal government agencies on the topics of team building, conflict coaching, peer coaching, conflict resolution, employee evaluations, performance reviews, leadership, and a variety of other pertinent topics supporting U.S. federal employees and leaders.

John has written and cowritten numerous articles and books, including a two-year series supporting new principals for the NAESP publication, *Principal*, and *Effective Group Facilitation in Education, Working With and Evaluating Difficult School Employees, So Now You're the Superintendent!, Energizing Staff Meetings, Creative Strategies to Transform School Culture, Thriving as a New Teacher, Score to Soar, Achieving Great Impact, Working With Difficult and Resistant Staff,* and *Flip This School.*

John earned a doctorate in educational leadership and policy studies from Loyola University Chicago and a master's degree in educational leadership from the University of Nebraska Omaha.

To learn more about John's work, visit his website at ellerandassociates.com, or follow him @jellerthree on Twitter.

Tom Hierck has been an educator since 1983 in a career that has spanned all grade levels and many roles in public education. His experiences as a teacher, an administrator, a district leader, a department of education project leader, and an executive director provide a unique context for his education philosophy.

Tom is a compelling presenter, infusing his message of hope with strategies culled from the real world. He understands that educators face unprecedented challenges and knows which strategies will best serve learning communities. Tom has presented to schools and districts across North America with a message of celebration for educators seeking to make a difference in the lives of students. His dynamic presentations explore the importance of positive learning environments and the role of assessment to improve student learning. Tom's belief that "every student is a success story waiting to be told" has led him to work with teachers and administrators to create positive school cultures and build effective relationships that facilitate learning for all students.

To learn more about Tom's work, visit his website at tomhierck.com, or follow him @thierck on Twitter or Tom Hierck on Facebook.

To book John F. Eller or Tom Hierck for professional development, contact pd@SolutionTree.com.

Introduction

Cassia, a sixth-grade student, has been in trouble for the last two years in school. In early elementary school, teachers commented about how attentive and interested she was in learning. All of that changed at the end of her fourth-grade year. She suddenly became withdrawn and quiet. She stopped turning in assignments and kept to herself a lot. Since it was the end of the school year, Cassia's teacher thought something had changed, but didn't want to pry into her family situation.

During fifth grade, all the classes were departmentalized. Cassia didn't make a meaningful connection with her teachers there and did just enough to get by.

For sixth grade, Cassia attended Floyd Middle School. At this school, the team members met every week to discuss the students and their educational progress. Floyd Middle School had adopted the care factor as a central component of its school culture. Principal Raul Haven had aligned resources to help teachers focus on students first. Teachers met in collaborative teams and structured each meeting based on the unique needs of the students and teachers.

At their third weekly team meeting, the team focused on student welfare. Team members could complete a referral and discuss student concerns at this meeting. The team members listened as Cassia's base teacher, Ms. Deacon, shared her concerns about Cassia.

After listening to her concerns, team members developed a plan to study the situation to better understand what was happening. They adopted the following elements in their plan:

- *As a sixth-grade team, they decided it would be important for each of them to develop a better relationship with Cassia.*

- *Cassia's base teacher, Ms. Deacon, would keep a log of Cassia's classroom behaviors to see if patterns had emerged.*

- *The collaborative team leader would keep Principal Haven sensitive about the data they had gathered so he could be ready to provide additional resources once the team better understood the problem.*

By implementing the plan, team members were able to develop a relationship with Cassia. As a result of this relationship, they were better able to determine the patterns in her behavior while also helping her to feel more comfortable and engaged in each classroom. After gathering more information, the sixth-grade collaborative team would meet again and develop a plan for implementing strategies to help Cassia to get back on track. The process would take some time, but the team knew Cassia needed the time to become comfortable with them.

In this scenario, the sixth-grade collaborative team put the success of their students at the center of their work. Because of Principal Haven's leadership, each collaborative team reserved at least one of their weekly meeting sessions to focus specifically on student welfare issues. Since this process has been implemented, the collaborative teams at the school have been able to keep many students from "falling through the cracks" and instead, helped them be successful. The leadership of Principal Haven had helped the school become more trauma sensitive.

Our Personal Experiences With Childhood Trauma and Leading Trauma-Sensitive Schools

As we detailed in our book *Trauma-Sensitive Instruction: Creating a Safe and Predictable Classroom Environment* (Eller & Hierck, 2021), we have experienced childhood trauma in our own lives, taught in classrooms using trauma-sensitive strategies, and led schools that served trauma-impacted students during our careers.

Because of our backgrounds and experiences, we are uniquely qualified to assist teachers and school leaders as they work with students from traumatic homes and situations. Our biographies appear at the front of this book, but following are some of the experiences we've had to directly transfer to the mission of supporting students, teachers, and school leaders in working with trauma-impacted students.

John F. Eller

In developing this book, John called on his extensive experiences in implementing foundational strategies that support trauma-sensitive classrooms and schools, plus his research and previous writings on the topic.

John has served as an elementary and secondary school teacher, a principal in several schools, an assistant superintendent of curriculum and learning, a principal's center director, a university professor, and in various other positions during his career. Following are some of John's pertinent experiences.

- Worked extensively as a classroom teacher, principal, and district office administrator in communities and neighborhoods that served students living in traumatic conditions.

- Supported teachers and leaders as a consultant in the areas of positive classroom environments, classroom management, building relationships, developing parent partnerships, and other areas directly related to adverse childhood experiences (ACEs).

- Developed and implemented programs that were beneficial to students experiencing trauma. One of his schools was honored with the Iowa First in the National Education (FINE) Award for transforming school culture, and John was named as the state principal of the year and a National Distinguished Principal with the U.S. Department of Education.

- Authored many books and articles on topics related to trauma-sensitive instruction, including developing the *care factor* with students and families, in which the principal helps teachers and students feel that someone cares for them; in turn, teachers show their level of caring for students, and then students show each other they care. This helps establish and maintain a caring and nurturing school culture. Topics also include school culture, classroom management, de-escalating conflict, and working with teachers to implement change.

- Worked as a consultant since 1996 with schools, districts, intermediate education agencies, and other education institutions on foundational topics related to trauma-sensitive classrooms and schools. In addition to consulting on these topics in North America, John also has worked with teachers and leaders in Chile, Australia, China, Japan, and Europe.

Tom Hierck

Tom has channeled all of his expertise and experiences into this new book to help teachers and leaders make their classrooms more trauma sensitive. Tom has served as a teacher, a school administrator, a program director, and an author in the area of trauma-sensitive teaching and leading. Following is a summary of those experiences.

- Worked extensively as a teacher, an administrator, and a consultant in the areas of trauma, behavior management, and developing student resilience and potential.

- Worked in programs serving students with severe behavior issues and in alternative education programs designed to help students experiencing trauma.

- Developed a model program to help indigenous students and families.

- Led the reform of a behavior program that helped students to build resilience, and implemented intervention programs, such as positive behavioral interventions and supports (PBIS), to help teachers understand the trauma behind behaviors and teach students alternative behaviors while building resilience.

- Worked as a consultant in North America and Australia helping educators understand student trauma, building classrooms and schools that are more trauma sensitive, developing classroom environments where students are taught and practice productive behaviors, building positive learning environments, and championing the idea that *all* students can learn and be successful at high levels.

- Authored many books on response to intervention (RTI), school and classroom culture, assessment, and positive behavior management all related to trauma-sensitive teaching and leading.

Both of us have had experiences similar to those many of your students may have had. This has been a tremendous asset in our work with students from traumatic situations. These experiences have helped us *relate* to them and understand some of what they are going through themselves, allowing us to empathize and step back and try to understand each situation in a unique manner.

Some of you may also have experienced trauma as a child. Somehow, you may have overcome your situation, or maybe the experiences are hidden in your deep memory and influence how you think and process experiences. Your experiences may have made you more sensitive and aware of the impact of trauma on your students, or they may have made you less tolerant of some of the situations your students are facing. This lack of tolerance may lead someone to think, "I worked hard and overcame my traumatic situations. Why can't my students do the same?" In contrast, if your experiences have made you too sensitive, you may allow your students too much leeway so that they are unaccountable for their behaviors. Letting students get by with misbehaviors does not help them develop the resilience they need to overcome their trauma. Whatever your experiences have been, trauma does impact how you think about working with trauma-impacted students.

Teachers tell us that more and more students live in trauma and experience mental health challenges. We have observed how trauma-impacted students struggle to focus and learn. These issues impact the classroom and behavior management, and cause teachers to take time away from teaching and learning activities to address students' mental health needs. These traumatic home situations have been amplified during the COVID-19 pandemic.

You don't need to have experienced childhood trauma to empathize and understand students' perspectives. If you try to understand what students might be experiencing, that's a great first step. Being able to step back before reacting will help you better understand their situations and develop positive relationships that will help you work with them more successfully.

Purpose of This Book

In *Trauma-Sensitive Instruction* (Eller & Hierck, 2021), we discussed the topic of trauma from the classroom or teacher perspective. In this book, we focus on trauma from a school and school leadership perspective. You'll explore ideas and strategies to support teachers and implement trauma-sensitive instruction as a whole school. Effective implementation and change happens because leaders help set the stage and promote and support these changes.

School and Classroom Focus on Trauma

At the time we were writing this book, the world was struggling to recover from the COVID-19 pandemic. Many educators were working with students who had returned to school from traumatic situations and experiences. Teachers were also dealing with great stress and complications related to teaching and learning. Trauma is not new, but the pandemic provided a clear focus on this element of life.

Throughout human history, people have experienced situations that caused trauma. Research related to situations faced by soldiers in the U.S. Civil War were highlighted in an article by M. Shelley Thomas, Shantel Crosby, and Judi Vanderhaar (2019). Upon their return home, soldiers showed signs of the traumatic situations they faced in battle. Some people thought the soldiers were overreacting or too sensitive. For several years, trauma treatment was confined to clinical settings, support groups, and other treatment options (Thomas et al., 2019).

Youth trauma and its importance became more prominent recently, in part, due to the work of Vincent J. Felitti (2019). Over several decades, Felitti studied the impacts of trauma on health well-being and wrote numerous articles supporting this work. His research has helped educators see the impact of trauma on their students. Because of this work, there is consensus around the idea that childhood trauma has long-lasting health impacts on adults. Becoming aware of the impact of trauma outside the school setting has made educators look beyond simple causes behind misbehaviors and try to determine if trauma outside of school influences behaviors that may be visible in school.

In working to understand the situations that some students face, it may be hard to feel how difficult these situations may be and how hard it is to concentrate. Later, as we examine how the human brain typically responds to trauma and stress, you'll see how the entire cognitive processing can be shut down or taken hostage when a student is trying to cope with a traumatic experience.

In our work over the years supporting educators dealing with trauma-impacted students, some have shared comments about their students such as, "I don't understand why he acts out like this," or "Why doesn't she feel she can share her situation with me? I think we have a good relationship." Many of these same educators also told us they grew up in relatively safe and stable homes. They said they did not have to worry about a drunk parent coming home and beating them up or coming home to an empty house and having to take care of their siblings because their parent was out partying.

Educators need to consider what students are experiencing in their traumatic situations. It is an advantage for you if you can empathize with them; doing so, you walk in their shoes. Pairing the strategies and techniques of developing trauma-sensitive instruction with the ability to try to understand the trauma is a powerful combination in working successfully with trauma-impacted students.

How Our Experiences Are Helpful to School Leaders and Teachers

We shared our backgrounds so you can see our unique perspective on the topic of childhood trauma and the importance of trauma-sensitive teaching and leadership. We understand what it's like to come from homes where traumatic experiences are a regular occurrence. We know how embarrassing it is to have a parent attend a conference with alcohol on their breath. We understand how hard it is to make up a story about how we got a bruise or why we can't have friends over to our apartment because of the situations that may be occurring there.

We moved beyond the situations that we lived in and moved away from them. We decided to become transition figures in our families to make sure we didn't continue to pass on the abusive situations we had experienced to our families and children. Hopefully, we were able to break the cycle of abuse and trauma and avoid subjecting our families to it.

We also decided to use our experiences and make a difference in the schools we have led. While we were growing up, teaching, and leading schools, there were few resources available to understand and lead trauma-sensitive schools. As leaders, we quickly saw differences in how teachers worked to support their students. Some teachers focused on bringing out the best, while others focused on content or compliance. Some teachers centered their classroom around the students, while others focused on imposing order and structure. Some teachers focused on building relationships and bringing out the best in their students, while others did not invest in these aspects.

As we spent time observing these relationship-oriented teachers, we made note of the strategies they used to accomplish building relationships while developing student thinking, problem solving, and increasing their academic skills. We wanted to learn the secrets of these great teachers so we could pass these techniques onto other teachers. By helping all teachers learn and implement these techniques, we found that all students could learn and grow in supportive classrooms.

Original ACEs Study

In *Trauma-Sensitive Instruction* (Eller & Hierck, 2021), we discussed the original ACEs study, which outlines the physical and mental damage that early and constant exposure to trauma causes in children and how it carries into adulthood.

The initial focus on ACEs started in the 1990s with a study cosponsored by the Centers for Disease Control and Prevention (CDC), and the health insurance company, Kaiser Permanente (CDC, 2020a; Felitti et al., 1998). This initial study examined the early experiences of approximately 17,000 middle-class adults. The study participants were asked to respond to a questionnaire, which requested they identify their experiences with adverse, stressful situations. This initial ACEs survey included experiences such as substance abuse in the home, parent incarceration, neglect of basic needs, and others. (Visit www.cdc.gov/violenceprevention/aces /about.html to access the full ACEs survey.)

The initial results of the original ACEs study are staggering. Almost two-thirds of the study participants had experienced at least one of the adverse experiences listed. More than one in five participants had experienced three or more adverse experiences. Additionally, those with higher ACEs scores had more health challenges as adults. Truly, their childhood experiences impacted their lives as adults (CDC, 2020a).

Additional studies on children also have been conducted. Data from the National Survey of Children's Health from 2011–2012 (as cited in Lu, 2017) show that nearly 35 million children experience at least one source of stress. Helen L. Egger and Adrian Angold (2006) find that children between the ages of two and five have experienced at least one type of severe stressor in their lifetime. Researchers and mental health professionals are concerned about the high number of children experiencing at least one stressful situation but are even more concerned about those experiencing multiple stressors. When children experience multiple stressful events, it has a cumulative effect. These cumulative effects cause multiple problems for children and teachers (Terrasi & de Galarce, 2017).

Based on these data, it is more important than ever to understand these traumatic situations and make classrooms and schools more trauma sensitive. This has been heightened by the world's struggle with the recent COVID-19 pandemic. With students and families working and learning from home, the traumatic situations students are facing have increased.

Because of the prevalence of childhood trauma, we decided to write this book to help school leaders understand the importance of this topic and share strategies and ideas to help move a school closer to being trauma sensitive. While there are many books on the trauma-sensitive process, none of them offer the unique perspectives and experiences that we bring to this topic.

Overview of This Book

This book is designed to serve as a resource as you embark on your trauma-sensitive journey. While information is organized sequentially, you do not have to read this book from cover to cover. Feel free to read the chapters in the order that makes the most sense for you. Following is an overview of the information you will find in each chapter.

- **Chapter 1: Examining Trauma and Its Impact on Educators and Students**—Chapter 1 examines both foundational and current information related to trauma and how it impacts the students, parents, and teachers in your school. The focus may need to be refined when working with teachers who have experienced childhood trauma versus working with those who have not. This chapter also explores recent brain research related to trauma, what it does to students' brains, and how it can shape their reactions. This information is important because it not only helps you understand what's happening to students, but also provides the information you need to design strategies to support students when coping with trauma.

- **Chapter 2: Fostering a Trauma-Sensitive Attitude and School Culture**—In this chapter, the importance of understanding the attitude and mindset you bring to school is crucial. If you have preconceived notions about students and their families that are experiencing trauma, your trauma-sensitive efforts will not be successful. Shaping your attitude as an educator and leader, and helping teachers to shape their attitudes, will help you move toward leading a trauma-sensitive school. This chapter also explores the concept of ensuring a culture of safety at school, so that all students feel supported.

- **Chapter 3: Creating a Stable and Predictable School Environment**—In this chapter, you will learn about some of the practices that can help a school become trauma sensitive. These practices are focused on teacher-level strategies that you can support though your leadership. You'll also learn how to help teachers establish and sustain a productive classroom culture that supports trauma-sensitive practices.

- **Chapter 4: Building Relationships With Parents and Families**—In chapter 4, you'll learn your unique role in reaching out to parents and families to help them understand and support your trauma-sensitive efforts. As a school leader, your influence goes well beyond what happens within the walls of the school. Building awareness and support is essential in helping you move your school toward becoming a trauma-sensitive community and a place for *all* learners to be successful.

- **Chapter 5: Building the Foundation for a Trauma-Sensitive School**—Moving from a traditional focus to a trauma-sensitive one involves building a foundation that you can use to shore up your trauma-sensitive implementation. In chapter 5, you'll learn how to establish a sound foundation to help you be successful on your journey to becoming a trauma-sensitive school.

- **Chapter 6: Planning the Trauma-Sensitive Journey for Your School**—In chapter 6, you will learn ideas and strategies to plan the trauma-sensitive journey for your school. Effective planning is key to success, and the strategies presented in this chapter will help you as you prepare and plan that journey.

- **Chapter 7: Launching and Sustaining Trauma-Sensitive Practices in Your School**—Chapter 7 details ideas and strategies to help ensure the successful launch of trauma-sensitive implementation for your school. It outlines some aspects you will need to pay attention to and address on the start of your journey, plus some important strategies to maintain and sustain the changes related to trauma-sensitive practices.

Conclusion

As you review the information in this book, we hope you find specific strategies and techniques to meet your needs and fit the trauma-sensitive culture you are trying to establish at your school. The work will be hard but well worth the effort in helping trauma-impacted students move beyond their situations and transition to stop the cycle of trauma for themselves and their families.

In this introduction, we outlined some basic information for you to consider as you begin to address the issue of trauma and positive mental health in your school. As you read through the book, you'll find positive and productive strategies you can implement to support student growth and success. This journey may take some time, but ultimately, it has the power to improve the lives of your students both in and out of school, now and in the future.

chapter one

Examining Trauma and Its Impact on Educators and Students

Michelle, an eleventh-grade student at Powell High School, seems to be angry and upset in school. She doesn't make eye contact with many of her peers and looks away when teachers call on her. When she does answer her teachers' questions, she speaks in short phrases and a low voice. Several times a week, Michelle gets into some sort of argument with one of her teachers, who sends her to the office. Normally, on her way out the door, she'll make some sort of negative remark like, "Good, I don't want to be in your (expletive) class anyway!" or "I don't give a (expletive) about this class and never want to come back!" Once Michelle arrives at the office, she is out of control and upset.

One of the assistant principals, Ms. Juarez, is good at connecting with Michelle and helping her calm down. When Ms. Juarez sees Michelle come to the office, her first response is to get Michelle to a safe spot where she can calm herself and reflect on the situation that just happened in the classroom. Once Michelle has had a chance to calm down, she and Ms. Juarez can talk and process the incident. Ms. Juarez uses these strategies to help Michelle get out of her trauma mind and back into her thinking mind.

In this scenario, it's easy to see how Ms. Juarez understands the impact trauma has had on Michelle and uses her understanding to help Michelle temper her reaction and get herself back on track. Ms. Juarez's response to Michelle is always consistent and predictable. This consistent response is important, and Ms. Juarez has provided training and development in the techniques to her administrative assistant and other office staff in case she's not available. That way, Michelle receives a safe place to calm herself and get her emotions back under control.

School leaders set the tone and develop the school's culture to help students be successful. As more and more students come from homes where they are experiencing traumatic and stressful situations, it is even more important for us to lead schools where the culture promotes success.

Understanding the impacts of stress and trauma on students can help you establish and maintain supportive school cultures and lessen their impact in the classroom. This is especially important in your role as leader, modeling and helping teachers expand their skills. In this chapter, you'll learn about the following.

- Definitions of *trauma* and *complex trauma*, and how these conditions impact students and classrooms

- Recent statistics illustrating the prevalence of childhood trauma in society

- An awareness that you and your teachers may have experienced early childhood trauma and how these experiences may affect your or their ability to work with trauma-impacted students

- Brain functions and impacts of trauma on the brain

Early childhood trauma has been called "the public health crisis of the 21st century" (Centers for Disease Control and Prevention, 2020b). Not only does it cause problems with students, but left unchecked, it is one of the leading causes of adult illness, depression, alcoholism, and a variety of other problems (Merrick et al., 2019). Making your school more trauma sensitive is one intervention that can lessen the impact of these traumatic situations.

Trauma Defined

As you think about how to lead a trauma-sensitive school, it's important to have a clear understanding of the concepts related to trauma, the potential causes of trauma, and the impacts you and your teachers may see as a result of trauma. We included some information here from *Trauma-Sensitive Instruction* (Eller & Hierck, 2021) to provide a foundation of understanding of that core content.

Childhood trauma can set the tone for difficulties in school. Kathleen Fitzgerald Rice and Betsy McAlister Groves (2005) offer the following definition of *trauma*: "Trauma is an exceptional experience in which powerful and dangerous events overwhelm a person's capacity to cope" (p. 3). The preceding definition contains key descriptors that communicate the impact of trauma, including *exceptional, powerful, dangerous,* and *overwhelm.* All these terms taken together convey a sense that some of the experiences of your students are well outside the boundaries of normal.

The impact of trauma can be different for each person. Trauma is an emotional experience that directly impacts each student in a slightly different manner but has a definite and lasting impact on learning. Kristin Souers and Pete Hall (2016) point out, "Our interpretations influence the degree of impact we feel following exposure to a traumatic event" (p. 16).

This important fact should help teachers shape how they interact with trauma-impacted students. Many students come from homes and neighborhoods where stressful and traumatic experiences can be regular occurrences. For example, according to Childhelp (n.d.), "A report of child abuse is made every ten seconds in the United States." Since the frequency of abuse is so common, many students must not have stable home environments due to experiences from direct abuse, neglect, and other situations in which there is constant stress. Teachers tell us that the constant stress and lack of stability mean students have difficulty calming down enough to feel safe and learn. Following are just some of the traumatic scenarios our teacher colleagues have reported students have told them or they have discovered in trying to help students learn.

- Alcohol abuse by an adult in the home

- Neighborhood violence

- Homelessness

- Single-parent homes (Living in a single-parent home itself may not cause stress, but complications, such as the parent holding more than one job, experiencing economic difficulties, dating, and other factors, may contribute to student stress.)

- A parent in prison

- Left home to take care of things while parents are gone

- Physical or emotional abuse

- Excessive responsibility for sibling care
- Observation of drug abuse
- Violence of one parent against another
- Multiple families living in the same home
- The victim of bullying
- In foster care
- Gang recruitment and gang violence

These and other constant traumatic events cause students to be on constant watch for their own safety. When they are worried about and reacting to violent environments or the fear of violence, it's hard for them to be able to relax and concentrate on thinking and learning. Given enough time in a traumatic environment, they can also begin to think trauma is normal and happens to others. This traumatic way of life can be hard to break out of or change when students get outside the trauma-filled environment.

Now that you've had a chance to gain some foundational information related to trauma, let's examine a scenario of a middle school assistant principal dealing with office referrals.

> In reviewing the office referrals over the last quarter, the leadership team at Pike Middle School notices a pattern. There seems to be an increase in office referrals for what Assistant Principal Harris would normally call minor offenses. These include things like not paying attention in class, talking back to teachers, incomplete work, and other issues that never used to get referred to the office.
>
> When Assistant Principal Harris talks with students during their referral visits, he notes that several disclose that they have a lot of stress and trauma in their homes. Several students also comment about how hard it is for them to re-learn how to "do school" after being home and in virtual learning for so long during the pandemic.
>
> Assistant Principal Harris decides to meet with the teachers who have been sending the majority of the referrals to gain their perspectives. In this meeting, several teachers also express the stress they are experiencing in helping students to acclimate back to school. They share that they feel pressure to help students catch up academically and have been pushing their students to work harder.

These teachers also relate that several students experiencing diffi-culties are telling them about some of the issues they experienced during the pandemic, including the deaths of close family members.

This scenario has been somewhat common as students and teachers returned to school after the initial COVID-19 pandemic. Students experiencing traumatic situations outside of school are stressed and disengaged from their learning. Teachers struggling to get students back into school and growing academically feel stressed and overworked. This level of stress sometimes causes them to overreact to the situations they may have been able to handle in the past.

Trauma that occurs outside of school can negatively impact both children and adults. If it continues unchecked, both the students and adults in the school setting can experience further difficulties. As school leaders, we need to be able to step back from the emotions and see the patterns of behavior occurring. Once we do, we can then make plans to help address the issues.

Original ACEs Study and Continued Prevalence of the Problem

The impact of trauma is something that teachers may have intuitively thought about for years. When we were students, it seemed that teachers had information about students' backgrounds and tried to provide positive experiences to counteract the trauma at home.

For example, when John was in seventh grade, one of his teachers invited him to join a fishing club. This teacher helped John get his first fishing pole and took him fishing. This experience gave John some temporary respite from his traumatic home experiences.

During this time in John's life, he did not share these traumatic experiences with others outside the immediate family. Most of the time, John felt he was all alone. Certainly, he never heard any of his peers or friends talk about these kinds of experiences. Traumatic family issues were kept private and hidden from others.

Even though some teachers were able to intervene, they had no comprehensive understanding of the impact of traumatic experiences on students or adults. There was very little understanding of the problem or its impacts.

We present information here about the original ACEs study so you, as a leader, can understand some of the commonly identified traumatic events and their impact on those you lead. In *Trauma-Sensitive Instruction* (Eller & Hierck, 2021), the original ACEs study was presented in relation to its impact on the students we serve in school. In our work with schools, many educators have reported that they, too, have had multiple ACEs in their childhood. Some of these educators also reported that their experiences impact how they react to trauma when they see it in the students they teach.

As you read, reflect on your own experiences and the potential experiences some of your teachers may have had with childhood trauma. Reflect on your attitudes and responses to issues in your school that may be related to trauma.

Since we wrote this book after the initial impact of the COVID-19 pandemic, we suspect there may be even more impacts related to trauma affecting both students and adults. As issues arise in the students and adults you work with, consider that some of these might be attributed to trauma associated with the experiences during the pandemic.

As noted in the introduction, in the late 1990s, scientists began to examine the effects of childhood trauma on adult health. The CDC and Kaiser Permanente conducted a collaborative research study that examined approximately 17,000 subjects identified as middle-class adults (CDC, 2020a; Felitti et al., 1998). Participants received a survey, which included a list of ten traumatic events. They were asked to rate which events they experienced before age eighteen. These traumatic events were called *adverse childhood experiences*. The original list of these ACEs includes the following (CDC, 2020a):

- Abuse

  - **Emotional abuse:** A parent, stepparent, or adult living in your home swore at you, insulted you, put you down, or acted in a way that made you afraid that you might be physically hurt.

  - **Physical abuse:** A parent, stepparent, or adult living in your home pushed, grabbed, slapped, threw something at you, or hit you so hard that you had marks or were injured.

  - **Sexual abuse:** An adult, relative, family friend, or stranger who was at least 5 years older than you touched or fondled your body in a sexual way, made you touch his or her body in a sexual way, or attempted to have any type of sexual intercourse with you.

- Household challenges

  - **Mother treated violently:** Your mother or stepmother was pushed, grabbed, slapped, had something thrown at her, kicked, bitten, hit with a fist, hit with something hard, repeatedly hit for at least a few minutes, or was at any time threatened or hurt by a knife or gun by your father (or stepfather) or mother's boyfriend.

  - **Substance abuse in the household:** A household member was a problem drinker or alcoholic or a household member used street drugs.

  - **Mental illness in the household:** A household member was depressed or mentally ill or a household member attempted suicide.

  - **Parental separation or divorce:** Your parents were ever separated or divorced.

  - **Incarcerated household member:** A household member went to prison.

- Neglect

  - **Emotional neglect:** [Nobody] in your family helped you feel important or special . . . [or] loved, people in your family [did not look] out for each other or [feel] close to each other, and your family was [not] a source of strength and support.

  - **Physical neglect:** There was [nobody] to take care of you, protect you, and take you to the doctor if you needed it, you didn't have enough to eat, your parents were too drunk or too high to take care of you, and you had to wear dirty clothes.

The results were surprising. As noted previously, of the 17,000 participants in the study group, almost two-thirds reported that they had experienced at least one ACE, while more than one in five participants reported that they had experienced three or more ACEs (CDC, 2020a).

The original ACE study was mainly designed to examine relationships between adverse childhood experiences and adult-level health issues. The high prevalence of ACEs in the adults in the study may have been surprising to some people.

Since the original ACEs study, there have been follow-up studies directly related to children. Here is some of the information from the follow-up studies.

- Nearly 35 million U.S. children have experienced at least one type of childhood trauma (Lu, 2017).

- Egger and Angold (2006) found children ages two to five had experienced at least one severe stressor in their lives.

- "Whether they work in a rural, urban, or suburban district . . . more than half of the students enrolled in public schools have faced traumatic or adverse experiences and one in six struggles with complex trauma" (Felitti & Anda, 2009, as cited in Terrasi & de Galarce, 2017).

Complex trauma involves experiencing more than two ACEs simultaneously. The effects of traumatic experiences multiply upon each other. If one in six students (or approximately 17 percent) are experiencing complex trauma, this is a high percentage of students who have complex traumatic experiences.

Teachers and school leaders we have worked with have found value in taking the ACEs questionnaire to determine their ACEs score. The original questionnaire used in the ACEs study (CDC, 2020a) included questions related to the health of the respondents since the study was examining longer-term health impacts related to ACEs. Figure 1.1 features an adapted version of the original questionnaire, focusing only on the ACEs components.

Completing the ACEs questionnaire yourself or having teachers complete it can be a valuable experience because it helps people identify their own situations and potential issues. It also can be problematic or challenging. Strong memories and emotions could be reopened for people who experienced ACEs in their earlier lives. Some of your staff might think that by taking the questionnaire, they will be asked to expose things about their past. Make sure you think about these and other potential problems before considering administering the ACEs questionnaire with staff. Keep the following in mind if you are considering asking your staff to complete the ACEs survey.

- **Emotional safety:** Thinking about issues from the past can be traumatic. Participants may not want to revisit issues they have left in the past.

- **Privacy:** Don't ask or encourage teachers to share their results. Keep the results private and confidential.

- **Potential issues:** Everyone deals with trauma in different ways. Don't assume a teacher who experienced complex trauma is going to need more support than a teacher who experienced a single traumatic event.

Use the ACEs questionnaire to raise awareness and understanding for trauma among your staff; however, use it carefully to reduce the negative aspects of opening up potential emotional wounds within your school.

Adverse Childhood Experience Questionnaire

Please review the following questions. Respond *yes* if this situation happened to you during your childhood (up to age eighteen) or *no* if it did not.

1. **Did a parent or other adult in the household often . . .**

   Swear at you, insult you, put you down, or humiliate you?

   Or

   Act in a way that made you afraid that you might be physically hurt?

   NO _____   YES _____

2. **Did a parent or another adult in the household often . . .**

   Push, grab, slap, or throw something at you?

   Or

   Ever hit you so hard that you had marks or were injured?

   NO _____   YES _____

3. **Did an adult or a person at least five years older than you ever . . .**

   Touch or fondle you or have you touch his or her body in a sexual way?

   Or

   Try to or actually have oral, anal, or vaginal sex with you?

   NO _____   YES _____

4. **Did you often feel that . . .**

   No one in your family loved you or thought
   you were important or special?

   Or

   Your family didn't look out for each other, feel close
   to each other, or support each other?

   NO _____   YES _____

5. **Did you often feel that . . .**

   You didn't have enough to eat, had to wear dirty
   clothes, and had no one to protect you?

   Or

   Your parents were too drunk or high to take care of you
   or take you to the doctor if you needed it?

   NO _____   YES _____

Figure 1.1: ACEs questionnaire.

continued →

Adverse Childhood Experience Questionnaire

Please review the following questions. Respond *yes* if this situation happened to you during your childhood (up to age eighteen) or *no* if it did not.

---

6. **Were your parents ever separated or divorced?**

    NO _____   YES _____

---

7. **Was your mother or stepmother . . .**

    Often pushed, grabbed, slapped, or had something thrown at her?

    Or

    Sometimes kicked, bitten, hit with a fist, or hit with something hard?

    Or

    Repeatedly hit for at least a few minutes or threatened with a gun or knife?

    NO _____   YES _____

---

8. **Did you live with anyone who was a problem drinker or alcoholic or used street drugs?**

    NO _____   YES _____

---

9. **Was a household member depressed or mentally ill, or did a household member attempt suicide?**

    NO _____   YES _____

---

10. **Did a household member go to prison?**

    NO _____   YES _____

Your ACEs Score

For all of the *yes* responses, score each one as a +1. Total up all of your +1 scores. That number is your ACEs score.

TOTAL *YES* RESPONSES: _____

Source: Adapted from Centers for Disease Control and Prevention, 2020a.

Impacts of Trauma on the Brain

Understanding the impact of trauma and stress on students can help you as you work with teachers to help them respond to student reactions from trauma, deal with classroom behavior situations, make adjustments in classroom processes and procedures, and other aspects of leading the transformation process to a trauma-sensitive school. This section is designed to provide an overview of brain functions.

Severe trauma, especially complex trauma resulting from multiple and simultaneous traumatic situations, can have a lasting impact on brain function and student learning. Trauma and traumatic events can have a negative impact on human brains. When children experience multiple traumatic events (complex trauma) or repeated traumatic events, they may continue to operate at a more "excited" state and not get a chance to return to their more normal, calm state in the short-term. Soon, these students can become either under-stimulated and not react, or over-stimulated and reactionary. Either reaction is not beneficial to learning and achievement in the classroom.

Physical Structures of the Brain and Trauma

To understand the impact of trauma on our learners, it's important to understand basic brain structure and function. Our brains have a couple of basic responsibilities. One is to protect us from danger. Another is to provide us with pleasure and satisfaction (Robbins, 1986). As we discussed earlier in this book, traumatic situations place humans in danger and work against gaining pleasure. In a traumatic situation, our brains try to remove us from the dangerous setting or experience.

In *Culturally Responsive Teaching and the Brain*, Zaretta Hammond (2015) presents a clear overview of the human brain and some of its functions. Human brains are composed of three layers that are stacked from bottom to top. In general, these layers function in a complex manner as they are added on top of another layer. They work both independently and in collaboration with one another in a coordinated manner. Let's look at the regions and functions in the brain and how each works to keep people safe.

The Reptilian Region

In *Brain-Based Learning*, Eric Jensen and Liesl McConchie (2020) outline basic brain functions. At the base of the brain in its lowest level are the brainstem and cerebellum. This region is often referred to as the *reptilian region* because the structures here are those that comprise the brains of most reptiles (Jensen & McConchie, 2020).

This brain region has limited thinking capacity and only reacts. Its major functions are protection and controlling automatic operations such as breathing, heart rate, blood pressure, and other functions that help keep people alive. Because it operates these automatic functions, it can also control them when people are in danger. This section of the brain also contains the medulla oblongata, which helps people to constantly scan their environment for danger (Jensen & McConchie, 2020).

In trauma-filled situations, the reptilian region of a child's brain reacts to the danger, bypassing the thinking and logical regions, and helping the child to escape the danger. This region of the brain helps children to react quickly, often without thinking, to protect themselves (Jensen & McConchie, 2020).

Students experiencing severe or multiple instances of trauma may come to rely on this reactionary behavior, and this reliance may spill over to the classroom. Since students' reptilian brains may be constantly scanning their environment for danger, small threats may trigger a reaction (Jensen & McConchie, 2020). By working to implement predictable, safe, and stable classroom environments, educators are trying to help the students to move their thinking to higher-level, more cognitive regions of the brain. This helps them become less reactionary. We'll talk about this aspect in more detail later in this chapter.

The Limbic Region

Stacked directly on top of the reptilian region is the limbic region. This is the region of the brain involved in emotion and processing emotional experiences. It helps the brain to learn from experiences and regulate emotions. While complex operations occur in this region, there are three major functions processed here: (1) coordinating communication and information processing; (2) holding short- and long-term memory; and (3) controlling and communicating emotions, such as fear (Hammond, 2015). We'll examine this region in more detail.

Hammond (2015) stresses the relationship between the *amygdala*, which is a component of the limbic region, and emotional processing. The amygdala sends a danger signal to the reptilian part of the brain and stimulates the release of the hormone *cortisol*. The release of cortisol in the brain effectively stops other brain functions, such as thinking and learning, which is called an *amygdala hijack*. According to Hammond (2015), "An amygdala hijack leads to our natural 'fight, flight, freeze, or appease' responses" (p. 40). (You may read more about these responses later in the chapter.)

When cortisol is present, the thinking parts of the brain are suspended or on hold. This is one reason why people under stress or in conflict may seem to be irrational. They may do things that don't make sense. Their brains cannot move to a cognitive or thinking mode until the cortisol level has decreased, enabling rational thought and processing (Hammond, 2015). According to Hammond (2015), "Cortisol stops all learning in the body for about 20 minutes and stays in the body for up to 3 hours" (p. 76).

Students experiencing trauma at home may come to school with significant levels of cortisol in their brains or systems. Even though teachers haven't necessarily been the cause of their trauma or stress, they can be the recipient of students' misbehavior as a result.

Let's see how Principal Allaway uses the awareness of the impact of trauma on the brain as he works with teachers to provide a stable and predictable environment.

> At the start of each day, Principal Allaway has the staff focus on building relationships with students and proactively look for students and situations that potentially may cause problems. During the classroom check-in process, students are able to assess their moods and take extra time to get ready for learning. As a part of the attendance process, teachers report students who assess their mood as "not ready for learning" or "I need time to myself." Principal Allaway connects with or has counseling staff connect with students who assess themselves in these categories more than two to three times per week. These interactions are designed to connect with and not punish students.
>
> Principal Allaway also engages the instructional coaches in supporting teachers as they work to refine their classroom environments to provide more stability and predictability. As he completes classroom walk-through visits, he also positively reinforces teachers when he sees them implementing stability strategies. He devotes one faculty meeting each month to discussing and problem-solving implementation of the changes in the environment of Highpoint. Many of these faculty meetings are led by the Highpoint Middle School leadership team so teachers feel empowered and engaged in the change process.
>
> While these school climate changes take time, they are gradually becoming part of the culture of the school—a new way of working that's good for all students, but especially students coming from trauma-impacted backgrounds.

In this scenario, Principal Allaway had his staff focus on a small number of changes and then followed through to make sure they did what was expected and received his recognition and support. In making school changes related to trauma-sensitive instruction, begin by focusing on elements related to stability, consistent procedures, and helping keep the atmosphere calm. Once you have helped staff to create a stable and predictable environment, you can work on other elements of trauma-sensitive instruction.

Brain Responses to Trauma

Humans have always had some exposure to stress and trauma. In more primitive cultures, there were many physical dangers. People were exposed to attacks from wild animals, attacks from neighboring groups of people, danger within a social group or village, or a variety of other ever-present dangers originating in the natural and social worlds. As people organized themselves into more complex societies and became more specialized, some of the physical dangers in their lives may have diminished. Unfortunately, other stressors arose to take the place of some of the earlier physical dangers.

In addition to what seems like increasing opportunities for children to see and experience trauma personally, on television, and through social media, the COVID-19 pandemic also caused stress and trauma. In our work to support educators deal with trauma, they report that many of their students have shown impacts related to the COVID-19 experience. For example, one teacher shared that her current class of first graders has a lot of trouble staying focused and on task. They get frustrated easily and seem to lack the stamina to work for even relatively short periods of time. She said that for many of her students, this is their first school experience in almost two years. Middle school and high school teachers are reporting the same kinds of issues for their students.

According to Jensen (2013), "Aggression enables a student to feel in control and take charge of a situation" (p. 17). Many trauma-impacted students don't have any level of control in their home lives. Their acts of aggression and acting out can be a way for them to gain some control over their lives. We'll talk more about this idea in later chapters.

The prevalence of fears focused on physical harm was much higher in past societies. Physical attacks required quick and direct responses. If a person was being attacked by a wild animal, it was beneficial to take one of three actions: (1) fight, (2) flight, or (3) hide (Hammond, 2015). Human brains became accustomed to quickly making a determination of the best response and then communicating with the body to act out the decision. Making clear and quick decisions may have enabled people to survive.

As civilization changed over time, threats from natural sources may have diminished. We worry less about wild animal attacks, raising our own food, or other dangers of the past. Those fears and dangers have been replaced by more modern fears that include intimidation, threats, and so on. Even though the dangers are somewhat different than those of the past, human brains react to these new fears in a similar way.

Hammond (2015) outlines the typical danger response when the brain is under stress or attack. Fear activates the *amygdala*. The amygdala stimulates the release of *cortisol*, which stops learning and stays in the body for two to three hours after the stressful event is over. The release of cortisol leads to the fight, flight, or hide survival behavior. After a few hours, the body metabolizes the cortisol, and the person returns to a more normal state.

So, if students experience a stressful situation right before they leave home for school, that stressful experience may stay with them for two to three hours. During this time, it may be difficult or impossible for them to engage in learning. Their brain may be still communicating to them that they need to fight, run (flight), or hide. This is important to note since the time before school can be where issues and acts of violence occur. Some students can still be having a cortisol release in response to a traumatic incident at home in the morning. Providing safe and stable before-school environments can reduce the number of violent or aggressive incidents.

Shawn Nealy-Oparah and Tovi C. Scruggs-Hussein (2018) discuss two types of trauma: (1) *acute* (single event) and (2) *chronic* (continuous or multiple events). While both affect the brain, their long-term impacts are very different. If a student experiences an acute or single traumatic event, their brain releases cortisol, and the flight-or-fight response takes over. After the imminent danger or traumatic event passes, the student's brain returns to its normal state. Having dealt with the danger or traumatic event, the student may even develop improved coping mechanisms to address a traumatic event in the future.

On the other hand, if a student is experiencing chronic ACEs simultaneously or several on a regular basis, the student may be moving between the normal and arousal states, without the opportunity to remain in the normal, relaxed state. If the arousal state of the brain becomes the prevalent state because of multiple traumatic experiences or complex trauma, it can be hard for the brain to return to the normal, relaxed state (Nealy-Oparah & Scruggs-Hussein, 2018).

In the earlier scenario involving Michelle, she didn't have a chance to calm herself and move back to a normal state. As she moved from class to class, her arousal stayed high until she blew up and got kicked out of class. Ms. Juarez's strategy to provide Michelle a safe space for self-calming before she addressed the issue allowed Michelle to return to a more normal state.

As the school leader, it's important that you help teachers understand that when students experience trauma, they can take actions of fight, flight, or hide in response. Hammond (2015) introduces two additional responses—*freeze* or *appease*. These responses are important for teachers to understand so they can identify that some behaviors are based on these trauma responses and not necessarily directed at them. "Don't take it personally" or "It may not be about you" are two important thoughts to keep in mind when working with teachers of trauma-impacted students. In order to help teachers to understand these responses, it's important for you to understand and be able to explain them.

As noted earlier, Hammond (2015) identifies five responses children might have to experiencing trauma: fight, flight, hide, freeze, or appease. Let's examine each of these five responses and how they can impact students in the classroom.

Fight

During the fight response, children stand their ground and fight back in traumatic situations. In fighting back, children are hoping they can remove the trauma by matching power for power. If a child is facing an intoxicated parent who becomes abusive, that child may fight back to make the adult stop or see that the child will be a formidable match, causing the adult to back off or move away. Some children's personalities will enable them to fight back right away, while others may need to have several traumatic episodes before fighting back.

Since the default response to match aggression with aggression may not be a part of the student's normal behavior, a teacher may not see that a student has this capacity to strike out if a situation that triggers this behavior doesn't regularly occur in school.

Flight

This behavior occurs when students try to get away or rapidly remove themselves from a traumatic situation. Flight behavior can occur when students think they are weaker or subordinate to the person responsible for the traumatic situation. The flight can be a physical behavior or mental in nature.

In the classroom, a student may actually get up and leave the learning situation. This flight from the situation may be the result of built-up in stress from ongoing trauma.

Hide

When a person exhibits the hide behavior, he or she may try to avoid traumatic situations by disconnecting or trying to become invisible. The hide behavior is a way for children to withdraw and not be noticed during a traumatic event. John demonstrated the hide behavior with his alcoholic parent. He would move away from the situation and hope nobody saw him. If his parent did find him, he would have to move to the flight-or-fight mode in order to deal with the situation.

In the classroom, students who have learned the hide behavior may seem to be daydreaming or withdrawn. They may not be able to answer questions when called on or easily connect with others. Confronting their behavior or calling them to attention will not make the situation better and may promote the hiding behavior instead.

Freeze

Closely related to hide is the freeze behavior. People who exhibit the freeze behavior in traumatic situations may stop and be unable to move. Apparently, their brain doesn't know what action to take, so they can't take any action at all. Many of you may have heard stories about people in the vicinity of a tragic incident who just froze. They couldn't leave or help the victim. After the traumatic incident passed, they wondered why they weren't able to act.

Hopefully, you won't experience the freeze behavior in the classroom, but you may see effects of it. Similar to the hide behavior, students may daydream or zone out in response to a traumatic situation. They may not remember what happened in relation to an abusive situation. When you notice students excessively daydreaming, it may indicate something traumatic has happened to them. Providing an atmosphere where students feel safe and supported may be the best way to help them work through these experiences.

Appease

Children may have learned that the best way to respond to, or try to remove, a traumatic situation is to appease the person or persons inflicting trauma. When people appease, they try to determine what the person in power is trying to gain and then give them what they want in the hope of making the situation go away. For example, if a child is dealing with an alcoholic parent who is drunk and aggressive, agreeing with that parent, doing what the parent asks, and so on, can often decrease the parent's aggressive behavior.

In the classroom, you may see students who constantly give in to others or let others push them around. This can create situations in which some students dominate others. If this behavior continues over time, the student exhibiting appeasing behavior can become even more of a victim in the future.

How Personal Experiences With Trauma Can Shape Reactions

Because the prevalence of ACEs in the general population is so high, there's a good chance that you or your staff may have had your own experiences with ACEs. In some cases, your own direct experiences with ACEs can make you compassionate or more understanding of the conditions some students may be experiencing. On the other hand, having seemingly survived ACEs can make some teachers less compassionate or understanding of these students' situations. Some teachers think that since they developed resilience and overcame adverse experiences, others should be able to as well. Thinking like this may make these teachers less empathetic and understanding as they encounter and work with students to build resilience and overcome the impact of ACEs.

In working with teachers and school leaders, we've had people approach us during seminars to share their childhood traumatic experiences. One assistant principal told us that he didn't have any of the traumatic experiences identified in the ACEs survey.

He said the lack of these experiences may have made him less understanding of some of the situations he encounters in working with students. In another case, a teacher told us she had experienced three of the traumatic experiences from the ACEs survey. She said that she has to be careful to balance her empathy (understanding) with her feelings of sympathy (feeling sorry) for students impacted by trauma.

Knowing that both extremes may be harmful to students, you will need to monitor your attitudes, perceptions, and responses when working with trauma-impacted students. In a leadership role, you need to not only monitor and adjust your feelings and attitudes, but also understand and try to positively shape teacher attitudes and behaviors. As a school, the instinct to make allowances for traumatic situations must be balanced with the limited (or zero) tolerance school districts have toward violence or other negative behaviors.

You may also find it helpful to discuss the aspect of educator experiences and reactions to trauma-impacted students. Allowing teachers to openly talk about these issues can help them work through some of the emotions and reactions they may encounter as they work with trauma-impacted students. Figure 1.2 shows a staff meeting agenda for what this sort of conversation might look like.

1. Welcome and share good news: Build in the strategy of having teachers share good news to help set the tone for a productive meeting.

2. Review or initial presentation of ACEs study: Discuss the ACEs study and stress the impacts of ACEs on the brain.

3. Discuss the impacts of ACEs on students: Discuss your own reactions to stress and earlier ACEs. Leaders and teachers may choose to share.

4. Discuss how your reactions to student trauma could be impacted by your own ACEs or stress experiences.

5. Brainstorm strategies you might use to help moderate your responses to stress and adverse childhood experiences (for example, forming adult support groups, learning and practicing temporary suspension of opinion, developing self-care strategies).

6. Develop a plan to implement, monitor, and refine reaction moderation strategy implementation.

Figure 1.2: Sample faculty meeting agenda for conversations related to trauma.

Let's see how a faculty meeting using some components from the agenda in figure 1.2 might look in the following scenario.

At Bella High School, the teachers have noticed a change in the students during the current term. Many teachers comment that they observe a significant number of students being either less engaged in class or more easily distracted. Several teachers share their concerns with Principal Abbott. She decides that it would be a good time to have a problem-solving meeting to discuss the issue and develop a plan to address the situation.

In the meeting, Principal Abbott starts by placing teachers in small groups to discuss the issues they are facing. As each group reports out, Principal Abbott writes their concerns on chart paper. She then asks the groups to discuss the recent trauma-sensitive professional development session they attended and to address how trauma might be impacting student behavior. The groups come to the conclusion that traumatic situations outside of school may be impacting student behavior and engagement. They also discuss how their own traumatic situations may be impacting students. The teachers develop a strategy to informally assess the student "mood" as they welcome students to their classrooms.

In her high school literature class, Ms. Sinehouse knows several of her students come from homes where stress and trauma are regular occurrences. She always greets her students at the door at the beginning of class and informally assesses their moods. As she makes note of students' moods, she thinks about how she may react if they get off task. Ms. Sinehouse has experienced her own trauma so she knows that she may need to resist her temptation to feel sorry for or lower her expectations for these students. By informally assessing students when they come into her classroom, she can start to think through possible interventions before incidents happen. She can mentally prepare for potential issues.

In this scenario, Principal Abbott decides to meet with her teachers to address this important issue. If she had waited for the situation to get worse, the teachers may have just reacted to this issue by flooding the office with referrals. Instead, Principal Abbott is able to help them develop a plan. Once implemented, they can gather data about the plan to see how it is working.

As school leaders, it's important that you care for your staff and think about how some of their behaviors may be the result of trauma—either childhood or ongoing. In *Working With Difficult and Resistant Staff* (Eller & Eller, 2011), the authors discuss the importance of trying to understand what might be making or contributing to staff members' difficulty or negative behaviors and attitudes *before* deciding how to intervene. Be sure to consider the potential of trauma experienced by staff members as you embark on your journey to becoming a trauma-sensitive school.

Conclusion

In this chapter, we discussed ideas to help you understand and help manage the emotions associated with both trauma-impacted students and staff. We discussed several regions of the brain and their primary functions. We also examined the impact of trauma on the brain and the natural reactions people have when they are in dangerous or traumatic situations. As educators, it's important to have these understandings so we can spot the signs when they appear.

Understanding how the brain works and its reactions to trauma is helpful to all students. It's also helpful to understand your own possible responses to trauma and how that might impact how you interact with colleagues and students alike. The ideas and strategies you have learned here are just the beginning or tip of the iceberg. As you grow in your own professional practice of working with teachers to implement trauma-sensitive practices, you'll refine and develop many more.

In chapter 2, we take a closer look at two crucial elements for success in developing a trauma-sensitive school—fostering a trauma-sensitive attitude and school culture. These two elements help provide a foundation for the changes you'll make for your school not only to help trauma-impacted students, but to provide a better place for all students.

QUESTIONS FOR *Reflection*

As you think about what you learned in this chapter and how it can be implemented in your school, reflect on the following questions.

- How does knowledge of the major brain regions help you understand how trauma impacts student and teacher thinking and learning and behaviors related to trauma? How can you use this knowledge to help teachers understand your discipline issues and decisions?

- What is trauma? How do traumatic situations impact the brain?

- How is experiencing a single traumatic event different from experiencing complex trauma? Why would the aspects of complex trauma be important to know?

- How can your own experiences with trauma impact your work with students experiencing trauma? How can improving your own awareness help when working with teachers and students?

- Why is it a good idea to understand how teachers who have experienced (or who are experiencing) trauma may react when they encounter trauma-impacted students? How does improving your own awareness help you avoid possibly making traumatic situations worse for students?

chapter two

Fostering a Trauma-Sensitive Attitude and School Culture

At Prairie Middle School, teachers work together to make their school a place where children feel cared for and welcomed. Students are greeted by each teacher when they come into their classroom for instruction. Teachers provide spaces within their classrooms for students to go when they are feeling anxious or agitated, and they can return to the regular classroom area when they are more comfortable. They teach social-emotional skills within their content areas and have helped students learn and practice problem-solving and conflict resolution skills and have them practice them on a regular basis. When teachers experience negative reactions or behaviors, they stop to try and reflect on what might be causing them rather than reacting and escalating the situation. A majority of teachers view student discipline as a learning opportunity and try to help students understand how to replace what got taken away as a result of their behavior.

This is a complete 180-degree departure from how the school operated in the past. Five years ago, Principal McCray arrived. In that era, teachers had regular confrontations with students. Teachers said they demanded respect but didn't seem to show any respect to the students. The classrooms were teacher centered rather than student centered.

In this scenario, the way the staff at Prairie Middle School does business has changed dramatically. The school culture is now student centered rather than teacher centered. Rather than blaming students for behavior problems and issues, teachers work together to try to determine the potential causes and then address them.

Perhaps you've had this experience. A teacher complains about a student who seemingly disrupts class every day. The student is rude and disrespectful and causes more problems, chaos, and disorder than the rest of the class put together. Each passing day causes further resentment, and you notice that the teacher seems to be more negative and resentful every day. While you recognize that it is normal for the teacher to feel frustrated and angry, the solution does *not* lie in you simply removing the student from the classroom. Despite having a student who is ruining your teacher's year one day at a time, and despite his or her best efforts to stay positive, you know it affects every aspect of teaching. How does a leader manage to support all members of the team while also ensuring every student gets an effective education?

There is a solution, and it starts with realizing that it's not the student's fault. It also is not the teacher's fault. It begins with recognizing that somewhere along the line the student has been let down by some (or all) of the adults in his or her life. It may be the pain of abuse and neglect, the residue of poverty, hunger, or some other trauma discussed in this book. It may be that his or her home environment has been overly permissive. Often it manifests itself most severely when the student is in the presence of an authority figure who appears to be setting ground rules and giving directions. Remember, behavior is a form of communication, and adults need to be receptive to the message they are delivering. This is not about being a consequence-free school; it is about becoming a trauma-sensitive school.

Understanding that the behavior the teacher is witnessing reflects a student's desire to be understood, believed in, and given strong boundaries might make the student choose an alternative behavior as a response. A more productive and proactive option can replace anger, frustration, and resentment. Rather than having a stress-induced morning drive to school filled with dread, the teacher might instead be driven by purpose. This could make all the difference, and it doesn't require the teacher (or you, the leader) to lower his or her standards or fail to hold students (or staff) accountable. Changing how you see the situation and altering what you do in response will improve the outcomes. Once students see that the adults are on their side, and are authentic supporters in their corner, their behavior will begin to change.

Just as you recognize that changing your approach and attitude toward students (and colleagues for that matter) might yield a different response from them, this shift in attitude is often rooted in how you view things, or the context in which you view them. The path forward in adjusting your view is rooted in a very simple cycle that you might consider adopting and sharing with school staff members.

In this chapter, you'll learn about ways to help your staff build the foundation and attitude to begin the trauma-sensitive school journey. This foundation will help them see the vision and work through unanticipated "bumps" in the road on the journey.

As you read this chapter, focus on the following.

- Understanding the importance of developing a trauma-sensitive mindset and attitude

- Focusing on attributes that help shape the culture of a school to become trauma sensitive

- Learning key elements of moving a school culture toward becoming trauma sensitive, including consistency, collaboration, trust, and dependability, which help staff develop a common purpose and understanding

In some cases, school leaders may forget about the important aspects that help build the foundation needed for success. By keeping these considerations at the forefront, you will ensure you have a sound foundation to help your trauma-sensitive journey be a success.

The See-Do-Get Cycle

Wayne Hulley and Linda Dier (2005) offer an approach to understanding students and their behavior with the See-Do-Get cycle. The See-Do-Get cycle does the following.

> [It] explains that individuals or organizations get the results they deserve as a result of the things they are doing. What they are doing is based on their belief systems, habits, and culture; therefore, meaningful change results first from seeing things in a new way and then from taking different actions that lead to different and hopefully improved results. The culture will change. (Hulley & Dier, 2005, p. 58)

When individuals *SEE* what's going on, all kinds of new options for what to *DO* present themselves. Then the results, or what they *GET*, change.

Figure 2.1 illustrates the See-Do-Get cycle, which can be applied to any situation.

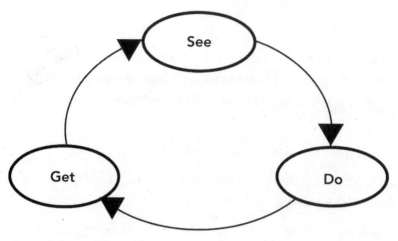

Source: *Hulley & Dier, 2005, p. 58.*
Figure 2.1: See-Do-Get cycle.

In response to the See-Do-Get cycle, Hulley and Dier (2005) suggest:

> With hope and its accompanying optimism, the results of actions taken will be viewed in a positive light. If goals are met, those who met them have good reason to be satisfied. If, however, goals are not met, those who tried to meet the goals can still learn a lot from the process and apply what they learn to future action. (p. 58)

As you consider the implications of shifting how you see things, it may be helpful to consider this model through the lens of leading a trauma-sensitive school or district. Even if we, as school leaders, have a general understanding of trauma, the global COVID-19 pandemic exposed on some levels that our response may not have shifted much as a result of the pandemic. In other words, we may still be processing this as an event similar to previous struggles we have seen in our schools, and educators might be responding the same way (regardless of how effective or ineffective the results may have been) and getting the same outcomes.

However, the impact of this event should cause leaders to see how this event is different than anything we've seen in education (at the writing of this book, we are in the third school year significantly impacted by the health crisis), suggesting we should take a different approach (for example, preparing for remote learning as a regular part of a student's journey in school), which would get a different result (less disconnected learning).

Principals should create an environment where all educators not only engage in trauma-sensitive action planning and action steps, but also ensure there is time for reflecting on the actions taken. School staff should embrace a collective commitment and examine where things are going well and where different or additional action is needed, resulting in different results than previously experienced.

Principals need to help teachers understand *why* they need trauma awareness. They should engage the faculty in professional development to engender a mindset shift and ensure all members know the brain science around trauma, as well as the potential effects of trauma on students' social, emotional, and academic development. They should provide professional learning for teachers to de-escalate a situation while also emphasizing the importance of adults to remain grounded and maintain self-control and empathy, and maximize the power of their relationships. Equally important is that effective principals recognize the need to support the adults as much as they expect the adults to support students. They must intentionally promote the notion of personal self-care and support it by building time throughout the year for educators to engage in the practice. They should provide support for teachers who are feeling overwhelmed and need immediate separation from the stimulus being provided by a student.

The Importance of Attitude

When we think about attitude, a favorite Zig Ziglar quote comes to mind: "Your attitude, not your aptitude, will determine your altitude" (BrainyQuote, n.d.b). The clear implication of this quote is that leaders have a choice to make before taking their next steps, and that despite overwhelming challenges, the path forward involves adopting a positive attitude. Let's be clear, however, that being positive doesn't guarantee a result (but being negative definitely does!). It is critical that you adopt a positive attitude and project that attitude, in order to make positive strides. Raymond Smith, Karen Brofft, Nicole Law, and Julie Smith (2013) suggest, "When leaders practice resilient behaviors, their actions are contagious because they model the way for others to act in similar ways" (p. 141).

Attitude must be driven by authentic belief and modeled by the leader to have the maximum impact. However, leaders can't be leaders if they do not have followers.

Leadership is about having social influence that extends the efforts of others toward achieving the goals of the team. In their book *Tribal Leadership*, Dave Logan, John King, and Halee Fischer-Wright (2008) talk about the leader being "someone who can unstick the conveyor belt—and make it run faster—for whole groups of people" (p. 9). The influence leaders have is not derived from position or title, but from the attitude they present, the actions they take, and the expectations they model. Leadership requires moral courage, as demonstrated through taking action, despite the risk of adverse consequences. Leaders must have the desire and the ability to discuss issues like health pandemics and racial equity to engender growth in their team and on behalf of all students.

Rushworth M. Kidder (2006) is a leading authority on moral courage and identifies three key elements of moral courage:

1. A significant danger (losing future opportunities or the team)

2. A willingness to endure (refusing to compromise)

3. A commitment to principle (equity) (p. 13)

Let's examine these three key elements through the lens of a school leader and in relation to a traumatic experience a staff member might experience:

> Elaine has been a foods and nutrition teacher for twenty-two years. When the COVID-19 pandemic hit, she adjusted all her teaching strategies to a remote learning platform. While she recognized this was never going to give her students the same experience as live food preparation, she was comfortable with this as she is the primary caregiver for her elderly mother. Her stress level has risen with the announcement that students and teachers will be returning to school for the next term. She worries about bringing the virus home to her elderly parent. She shows up for her first meeting with the principal wrapped head to toe in various articles of clothing and informs the principal that she will be teaching this way with most of the instruction occurring via video presentation.

This example offers many challenges if the staff perceived that the leader is not supporting a valued member of the school team. The loss of support may not be limited to one teacher but instead, could ripple out to the entire faculty. However, there are also the needs of the students, many of whom are seniors, impacted by remote learning that concluded their previous year of schooling. Elaine needs to be able to share the stress she feels and turn to the principal for help. While not backing away from the expectation of a quality education for all students (an issue of equity), the principal must demonstrate empathy while providing some level of support during these difficult times. This also highlights the crucial importance of recognizing the attitude and understandings you bring to the situation. The challenging times won't define the principal; it's the response to the challenging times that will.

Shaping your attitude as an educator and leader and helping teachers shape their attitudes will ensure your success as you move toward leading a trauma-sensitive school. As Kenneth C. Williams and Tom Hierck (2015) point out, "Our work with schools has illuminated one important point about what it takes to create school-wide cultural change: leadership is not a solo act" (p. 17). Implementing strategies to support a trauma-sensitive school requires a collective commitment and a positive attitude among all members of the team to implement the kinds of responses and changes needed to implement a trauma-sensitive school.

It is equally important to consider the concept of *implicit bias*, which is "an unconscious association, belief, or attitude toward any social group. Due to implicit biases, people may often attribute certain qualities or characteristics to all members of a particular group, a phenomenon known as stereotyping" (Cherry, 2020). Stereotyping affects your understanding, actions, and decisions in an unconscious manner. Human brains and bodies are designed to survive—and a useful tool for survival is being able to instantaneously sort things and people into categories such as *safe* or *dangerous*, *friend* or *foe*. This sorting occurs without an individual's awareness or control. Although we use the word *bias* here, leaders need to recognize (both in themselves and in their team members) that implicit biases are different from known biases that individuals may choose to conceal for social or political correctness. Implicit biases occur without awareness and aren't accessible through introspection. However, they are influenced by early life experiences, the media, and surrounding environments.

Stephen R. Covey (2013) summarizes the notion of implicit bias quite well: "We see the world, not as it is, but as we are—or, we are conditioned to see it" (p. 323). Each person has lived a singularly unique life and been exposed to a myriad of stimuli that have shaped the people they are today. The word *association* can provide a simple example of implicit bias. If you hear the word *bread*, what comes to mind first? It may be *butter* or *water*, depending on your background. The association may be different for an individual with different ethnic origins than your own. Unconscious racial stereotypes are a major example of implicit bias.

As leaders work with their teams and help soften some of these attitudinal dispositions, it is also important to recognize a few things about implicit bias.

- They are pervasive, and everyone possesses them, even educators who might profess impartiality.

- These implicit associations may not align with your stated beliefs or stances individuals explicitly endorse.

- They are malleable and can be gradually unlearned.

It is also important to be aware of the conditions that may exacerbate implicit bias so that, when these conditions exist, leaders can be extra vigilant to ensure that biases are kept in check. Some of these conditions may include:

- Stressful or distracting situations that provide educators with too much information at one time

- Situations that reduce cognitive processing—for instance, being tired or "on autopilot"

- Incomplete or ambiguous knowledge of a topic

- Lack of feedback and accountability

- Fear, which can take on various forms, including fear about job security, negative reactions, looking incompetent, or a myriad of things beyond an educator's control

As we experienced during the COVID-19 pandemic, which inspired educators to engage in deep discussions around equity, it's easy to fall back on familiar routines or familiar thinking. Hierck (2017) suggests, "It is critical to recognize that before cultural change can occur in any classroom, a teacher must desire this change and recognize that there is some value and need for it" (p. 9).

Our work has led us to schools all across the United States and Canada, as well as overseas, and inevitably we encounter educators who have lost the belief in the efficacy of attitudinal change. The root cause often varies. Has a teacher become disenchanted because of the failure of the latest structural initiative (that was built on a poor culture) in a long list of failures? Have cynical leaders and administration hampered a motivated teacher who was initially enthusiastic, but is no longer willing to implement cultural change? These cynics and blockers were most likely not those types of people during the hiring process. The longer we let individuals work through challenges individually, the greater likelihood of divergence rather than convergence on critical approaches to ensuring we become a trauma-sensitive place of learning. We run the risk of cultivating the cynics and blockers who drain our valuable time and energy.

Every person will go through challenging life experiences. Maintaining a positive attitude is not always easy during the hardest of these moments, and the energy stores of individuals get stretched. It may be easier to shoot down a school initiative rather than confront a personal challenge. Leaders play the important role of reminding colleagues and staff of the importance of a positive approach while also supporting them during the hard times.

A Culture of Safety

If you or your colleagues hold preconceived notions that trauma-impacted students and their families are somehow less important than others, or that they have caused their problems and need to find a way out of it themselves, your trauma-sensitive efforts will not be successful. As we know from personal experience, nobody asks for this or deserves to suffer. We know we cannot stop trauma from happening. What we can do is create a safe place for educators and students to learn and grow regardless of what might be happening outside of school walls.

Souers and Hall (2020) talk about the concept of a "culture of safety" to engage educators in thinking about being effective in teaching and learning through establishing an environment where everyone feels safe to voice their concerns and contribute to a positive learning environment. They believe this to be a critical element in helping students and educators develop effective coping skills and resilience. They suggest that a culture of safety is comprised of the following three elements: (1) safety, (2) predictability, and (3) consistency.

1. **Safety:** Students and adults arrive at an environment that is free of bullying, violence, and any other threat to their physical safety. They also have permission to be who they are—to be and feel vulnerable; to trust one another; to experience respect, celebration, inclusion, potential, uniqueness, and emotional freedom. Examples of this provision of safety are establishing connections with every student,

providing rituals and routines, and having protocols in place that communicate expectations and support.

2. **Predictability:** Stress responses are often heightened when faced with the unknown. When interactions, conditions, and expectations are predictable, students and adults are more likely to remain regulated. Predictable settings include an increased sense of trust, clear communication plans, proactive practices, and an unambiguous focus on the mission.

3. **Consistency:** A consistent environment also contributes to a culture of safety. One of the most critical elements of a consistent environment is having staff agree on procedures, policies, and practices for whole-school success. When staff consent to these practices, it means they agree to implement and support them. They see the practices as valuable and commit as a team to enforce them in their daily actions. This includes understanding the intent of their actions, the common language they use, a mantra that all students embrace, and a relentless attitude that everyone will be successful . . . no matter what. (Souers & Hall, 2020, p. 36)

As leaders, how would you work through each of these three elements? Being the leader of a trauma-sensitive school doesn't mean you have all the answers—it does mean you commit to being part of seeking a solution. The impact of the COVID-19 pandemic and the unrest brought about by systemic racism have provided some significant learning opportunities and brought to the surface challenges schools and districts might not have had to confront previously. Building a culture of safety is a step toward making meaningful progress, and that only occurs when leaders recognize its value.

From Safety to Trauma Sensitive

Let's try to conceptualize a trauma-sensitive school. Some common principles are fundamental across all types of trauma-sensitive organizations whether it be a community agency, a medical or mental health provider, or, in our case, a school. Leaders of trauma-sensitive organizations must build policies and practices that are well-aligned to the common principles. Policies such as those related to trauma screening, a social-emotional learning curriculum, personnel budgeting, and discipline must all be continually evaluated to ensure they stay in sync with the core principles of trauma-sensitive care. These practices—day-to-day operations, interactions, and instructional approaches—are truly what educators can control. The Substance Abuse and Mental Health Services Administration (SAMHSA; 2014) identifies six principles leaders need to focus on in order to support a trauma-sensitive school.

1. **Safety:** People don't feel safe after experiencing trauma, which results in focusing their resources on remaining in a hyper-vigilant state. Creating an environment where everyone feels physically and psychologically safe focuses resources on healing, learning, and healthy development. It's important to understand the meaning of *safety*, as defined by students and staff, not by your viewpoint as the leader.

2. **Trust and dependability:** Trauma can make people feel violated and betrayed, making it difficult to trust others and accept support. Fostering the development of relationships that are trustworthy and dependable provides an opportunity for people to begin trusting again. A key element of this principle is providing stability and predictability.

3. **An understanding of stress and trauma through peer support:** You can't know how to respond and support persons impacted by trauma until you understand the impact of stress and trauma. Through that understanding and peer support, your responses will be more effective and compassionate.

4. **Collaboration:** Trauma can make people feel alone and isolated. Healing happens in healthy relationships in which the approach is *power with* rather than *power over*. Everyone has a role to play in a trauma-sensitive approach. When trauma-sensitive practices are implemented with consistency and within a common language and vision, everyone is more likely to feel safe, trust one another, and engage in learning.

5. **Empowerment:** The experience of trauma takes away one's sense of power and control and leaves feelings of helplessness and hopelessness. By ensuring that everyone receives authentic opportunities to have their voices heard and their strengths recognized, you create an environment where people are empowered to advance healing and

well-being for themselves and others. Leaders must acknowledge historical and existing power differentials.

6. **Cultural humility and equity:** Diverse cultural groups may react to traumas and stressors differently and may experience differences in how others respond to traumatic experiences. Being open to understanding the trauma and adversity caused by historical, institutionalized, and societal oppression allows us to respond with cultural humility, work together to mitigate these harms, and enhance equity. Leaders should actively address and move past cultural stereotypes and biases, practice cultural responsiveness, leverage the healing value of cultural connections, and recognize and address historical trauma.

Conclusion

In this chapter, we examined the elements needed to build a foundation for change and success in your trauma-sensitive journey. Without these elements in place, you may find that your staff will not have the understanding and commitment to stay positive when they encounter issues during the journey. By considering and emphasizing these elements, you can help develop a positive school culture that is able to sustain and support change.

In chapter 3, you'll learn about one of the most important components in a trauma-sensitive school—creating a stable and predictable school environment. You'll discover how to support teachers in maintaining this consistency and predictability in their classrooms to meet the needs of *all* students, not just those who are trauma impacted.

QUESTIONS FOR *Reflection*

As you think about what you learned in this chapter and how it can be implemented in your school, reflect on the following questions.

○ Why is understanding trauma so important to the success of a trauma-sensitive school journey? What are some strategies you could implement in your school to build an understanding of trauma?

- Define the See-Do-Get cycle and how that model could help you refine the culture of your school. What are some things you can do to get the See-Do-Get cycle started?

- In moving from safe to trauma sensitive, how could developing the attributes of empowerment, trust, dependability, and collaboration help your staff work together on your trauma-sensitive school journey? What are some ways you could include these attributes in existing processes (such as team meetings)?

- Why is the classroom culture so important in helping all students successfully learn and grow, particularly those who experience trauma?

- What are some simple ways you can support teachers to develop a positive classroom culture that supports trauma-impacted students?

chapter three

Creating a Stable and Predictable School Environment

Principal Allaway has noticed that many of the students at Highpoint Middle School seem to be under stress when they first come to school in the morning. He also has noticed that quite a few discipline issues happen during homeroom or first-period classes. He decides to put a plan in place to provide a safe and stable environment for students.

His first step is to increase teachers' awareness of the issue of trauma and its impact on students in the morning. He provides professional development for his teachers on the impact of trauma at home and how it impacts Highpoint Middle School students when they first arrive at school. This professional development is also focused on the benefits of providing safe, predictable environments for students. During these sessions, some teachers are on board, but some are skeptical. Principal Allaway knows he'll need to follow up with them and support them as he moves forward to establish a safe and predictable school environment.

The second step is to set up a safe and predictable environment to focus on schoolwide processes. These are areas under his direct control and places where he can model the changes he will ask his teachers to do in their classrooms. Principal Allaway decides to play music as students enter the building to provide a calming effect. He allows students to enter the school when they arrive rather than making them wait outside as they have in the past. He provides supervision for students to come into quiet areas, such as the media center, the front commons, and a couple of larger classrooms, where students can complete their work. Principal Allaway and the staff want to build relationships with students as they super-vise these areas.

The third step in the process to make the environment more stable and predictable is to move stable processes to each classroom. Principal Allaway works with the Highpoint leadership team to develop a core set of classroom processes all teachers can imple-ment. These include:

- *Student self-check-in process*

- *Mood checks or self-assessment processes*

- *Quiet or thinking areas where students can go when needed*

- *Teachers informing the counseling center when they see or suspect a student may be having a bad day or may have experienced a traumatic incident before coming to school*

By implementing common practices and following through to sup-port teachers, Highpoint Middle School has seen a significant drop in office referrals and an increase in student achievement. Teachers are better able to teach and are less frustrated by situations they encounter in the classroom.

In this brief example, Principal Allaway focuses on three attributes of the envi-ronment to make Highpoint a stable and predictable place for trauma-impacted students: (1) increase teachers' awareness of the issue of trauma and its impact on students, (2) focus on schoolwide processes, and (3) move stable processes to each classroom. In this chapter, you'll learn how to support teachers in providing stable and predictable classroom structures that can benefit all students, including those who do not experience multiple or complex traumatic events outside school. The focus is on how you can use your skills as a leader to help teachers be successful in adopting these structures.

In this chapter, you also will learn the importance of encouraging and supporting teachers in providing a predictable and stable learning environment for students who experience trauma outside of school.

As you review the information in this chapter, be sure to focus on the following.

- The role that stable and predictable environments have in helping students' brains cope with trauma and move back into learning modes
- Ideas and strategies to help teachers develop stable and predictable learning environments in their classrooms and within the school that are trauma sensitive for all students

While establishing and implementing predictable and stable classroom and school environments won't fix every trauma-related problem, they go a long way in helping improve learning for trauma-impacted students, as well as their classmates. It's worth the effort to help *all* students be successful.

Classroom Considerations for Trauma Behaviors

As a school leader, your impact on students is mainly a result of your impact on the teachers you lead. This information in this section will help as you work with teachers to implement classroom and school-level strategies to meet the needs of all students, including those who are impacted by trauma.

While students may experience similar incidents of trauma (for example, neglect, abuse, and exposure to drug addiction), their reactions might be quite different. Two students may be experiencing verbal abuse at home, but one may be on edge and strike out when the slightest issue arises (fight response). The other may be withdrawn and avoid contact (hide or appease). The reaction of any trauma-impacted student could be unpredictable.

While it will be important for teachers to respond personally to each student, there are some foundational classroom structures that help trauma-impacted students feel support and a sense of trust, and also help increase their ability to learn in the classroom.

Teacher Attitude and Demeanor

In order to help all students be successful, especially students facing trauma, teachers need to have a positive attitude and a caring demeanor. Since educators teach children first and content second, the teacher's attitude is critically important. Students living in traumatic homes and experiencing emotional situations need unconditional support.

From 2000–2008, John worked with hundreds of teachers to develop their teacher leadership and action research skills. During his work, he conducted an activity in which he gave the participants a grid containing thirteen spaces. He asked group members to write in a significant memory from each of their thirteen (including kindergarten) years of primary and secondary education experiences. In all the groups, nobody identified content as their significant memory. All these teachers identified emotional connections they made with their teachers. The emotional connections and support are the most significant experiences students have with their teachers.

Like those teachers, John (growing up in a single-parent, trauma-filled home) also has significant memories of teachers who looked beyond his home life to see what was good and strong within him. They were able to not only teach John just social studies, science, mathematics, and physical education, but also help him feel welcomed and loved. His experiences of emotional connection with his teachers helped to shape John and how he planned to break the cycle of trauma with his own family. The attitude and demeanor of these teachers helped overcome the emotional injury caused by the trauma.

Think about why you decided to become a teacher initially and then why you decided to move into leadership. What gifts did you bring to make a positive impact on students' lives? In *Thriving as a New Teacher*, John F. Eller and Sheila A. Eller (2016) include several templates to help teachers reflect on their purpose and strengths. (Visit www.solutiontree.com/free-resources/instruction/tnt to find these helpful templates online.)

Classroom Culture

In *Seven Keys to a Positive Learning Environment in Your Classroom*, Hierck (2017) discusses the importance of the classroom culture in determining student success: "When seeking to develop a successful, supported collaborative learning community, teachers must first develop a positive classroom culture" (p. 9). We share this aspect of classroom culture to help you, as a school leader, see the connections between various classroom cultures and the whole-school culture.

Consider classroom culture as the way educators do business, embracing the common ideas that hold them together and the bottom line in how we work together as a learning community to help ensure everyone is successful. In classrooms that have strong, supportive cultures, students work together toward common goals, listen to, and respect each other. When an incident arises, students work together to address it so they can get back to their normal, collaborative, caring culture.

Even though both the student and the teacher *live* the culture of supportive, collaborative classrooms and schools, it is the teacher who helps establish, nurture, and strengthen this culture. Be sure teachers are aware of the power of classroom culture. Once teachers establish individual classroom cultures, you can bring them together to help further solidify the school culture as a whole.

As trauma-sensitive classroom cultures develop, their synergy contributes to the overall school culture. Let's revisit the scenario of Highpoint Middle School and how Principal Allaway works with his teachers to use the synergy from their classroom cultures to develop the culture of the school.

> As Principal Allaway continues to support his teachers while they are implementing processes and structures to make their classrooms safer and more predictable, he notices the way each teacher introduces and reinforces classroom processes and procedures. After all the teachers have started to implement these processes and procedures, he does walk-through visits to see them in action and praises the students for following them. For example, since one of the common procedures is a signal for attention, Principal Allaway uses the same signal when he needs to get students' attention. All the students are able to see that Principal Allaway knows the signal and expects everyone to use it.

> Principal Allaway schedules more frequent faculty meetings during the initial implementation period. The focus of these faculty meetings is to discuss and refine the implementation of common processes. He designs the meetings so they are interactive, breaking the staff into small discussion groups, asking them to identify positives and challenges they are experiencing in the implementation, and problem solving those things that aren't going well.

> As a result of all of the focus and support, the common procedures and processes are starting to take hold.

In implementing these common expectations and procedures, Principal Allaway is helping teachers refine the culture of the school. By spending time and providing the focus and support needed for success, he is helping ensure that the collaboration among teachers will become the way they do business in the future.

A Sense of Caring and Relationship

This aspect is similar to the attitude and demeanor discussed earlier but takes those aspects to a deeper level. Once you help teachers become clear about their purpose for teaching (and yours for leading), you can move forward and focus on how you can use that purpose to build positive and productive relationships with students and staff. While it would be difficult to have similar relationships with every student or staff member, developing some sort of relationship in which students and staff know leaders care and are looking out for them is essential.

In *Fostering Resilient Learners*, Souers and Hall (2016) describe the difficulty of maintaining relationships with students who have or are experiencing trauma: "Relationships are not easy. . . . Just managing 'normal' relationships with our friends, coworkers, and family can be challenging. When we bring trauma-affected students into the equation, the delicate nature of relationships stands out even more clearly" (p. 90).

Students experiencing trauma may resist developing relationships with adults because of the lack of trust they may have in the adults who have caused or contributed to the trauma in their lives. Teachers' relationships with each of their students may be different, and that's OK. The important thing is that they are aware of this need and taking steps to develop relationships with all students.

Predictable Structures

One characteristic of the traumatic situations some students face is unpredictability. They may not know when the drunk or drug-addicted parent, boyfriend, or other family member may come home and want to beat up on them. They may be neglected in one instance and taken care of in another. Their world could be out of their control. The somewhat random nature of their life can keep the defensive mechanisms of their brain on high alert all the time.

Classrooms and schools need to be places of emotional predictability and consistency. The stability of the environment allows trauma-impacted students to let their guard down and focus on learning. This is an area in which leaders can help teachers see the need for predictability and consistency in their classrooms. While teachers establish predictability in their classrooms, you can also develop it in some common areas and processes within the school.

Developing check-in procedures, having consistent strategies for dealing with issues, and operating a predictable schedule help *all* students, including those impacted by trauma, to focus on learning. The procedures need to match the needs of the learners and your own needs as a teacher or leader. In *Thriving as a New Teacher*, Eller and Eller (2016) provide a template to help teachers identify the needs of their students and their own needs based on their preferred teaching style to help establish the structure of their classroom. (Visit www.solutiontree.com /free-resources/instruction/tnt to find this template online.)

Movement

As discussed earlier, trauma impacts the brain in ways that are good for survival but not always so good for learning. When students experience repeated or multiple types of trauma, the introduction of flight-or-fight hormones (cortisol) can move brain functions from cognitive to reactionary (Hammond, 2015). When the brain either is in an arousal state or repeatedly experiences arousal because of trauma, it may be difficult for students to sit for long periods of time without movement. Helping teachers implement periodic and purposeful movement within their classrooms addresses the needs of not only trauma-impacted students but *all* students.

You've probably noticed that the strategies beneficial for trauma-impacted students are beneficial for all students. Offering periodic and scheduled movement opportunities allows students to burn off steam and stay focused. Incorporating movement into lessons on regular intervals helps to re-energize learning channels in the brain plus reduce boredom. You may have noticed that even a thirty-second stand-up-and-stretch break can work miracles in re-energizing students' attention spans.

If you are a leader in a secondary school setting, teachers might tell you that passing time between classes provides all the movement students need. While walking from class to class does energize students, it's not enough to help them burn off negative energy and anxiety and regain their focus on learning. You can help make teachers aware of students' need for movement by asking the following questions.

- How long could you sit in a professional development session or meeting without movement before you started to feel anxious?

- How much time would you like to see between movement opportunities or activities?

While there are many ways to incorporate movement in the classroom, those that are the least detailed or complex for your teachers to manage seem to make the most sense. These include:

- Standing up periodically to stretch
- Meeting with another classmate to discuss an aspect of the lesson
- Having students meet in small groups partway through the lesson
- Asking students to show their learning by holding up their papers, signaling with their hands, pointing, and other simple movements
- Asking students to vote on answers by moving to different parts of the room
- Taking a one-minute walk as a group around the classroom
- Using manipulatives in learning

The strategies your teachers choose to implement should match their teaching style (and personal comfort requirements) and student needs, and fit the culture of their classrooms. If they keep these aspects in mind, the movement will seem natural and a part of their instruction rather than something out of the blue that will confuse or even cause disruptions in their classrooms.

Reflection or Metacognition

An effective management strategy to share with teachers is to help students understand their own behaviors and allow them to process their thoughts and actions. You may know this skill as reflection or metacognition. It is especially helpful for trauma-impacted students because parts of their life may be irrational and out of control. They don't see much reflection in the people and situations that cause them trauma. They may move from one traumatic situation to another with no reason. Because of the constant or multiple traumatic situations many of them face, they may never get a chance to reflect on their own actions in the traumatic events.

In their book *Fostering Resilient Learners*, Souers and Hall (2016) emphasize that reflection can help trauma-impacted students think about where they are at in their own emotional response to trauma. These authors share a story about their work with one student. In this story, they ask the student to reflect on where he is in his thinking, using either the *upstairs* part of his brain (thinking and problem solving) or the *downstairs* part (reactionary and defensive). This analogy helps the student understand his mind state so he can move toward resolution of the situation. By offering students opportunities to reflect several times each day, teachers help students monitor their own mind states and gradually gain control of their emotions. Trauma-sensitive teachers use a variety of techniques to help students reflect on and report their state of mind during the day, such as the following.

- Ask students to write down their thoughts for a few minutes and then read their writings.

- Develop an *emotion meter* that students keep on top of their desks. During reflection time, students use markers or some other means to rate their emotions.

- Have students display laminated green, yellow, and red cards (like the ones used by sports referees) to show their mood or emotions. When a student displays a yellow card, the teacher knows to check in with the student to see what needs to be done to move back to the green card. If a student shares a red card, the teacher knows the student may need immediate attention or should move to a quiet location to get his or her emotions back in control.

- Offer midday classroom meetings (similar to morning meetings) that allow students to discuss and process happenings in the classroom that may be impacting their emotions.

You and your staff are only limited by your creativity in developing strategies to help students reflect on and take control of their emotions. Being able to manage emotions is one element of building resilience that trauma-impacted students need in order to keep themselves on track and avoid repeating their own traumatic experiences with others.

Classroom Structures and Processes That May Perpetuate Trauma

Effective school leaders help teachers periodically examine both the structures and processes they use in their classrooms to ensure that their environments are trauma sensitive. A trauma-sensitive learning environment means that the teacher has designed the learning environment to minimize its impact on continuing or extending traumatic situations for students. Providing opportunities and helping teachers examine their classrooms to ensure they are trauma sensitive can be difficult at first but helpful as they notice a change in some students' behaviors. Sometimes, you'll have to support and encourage them to stay the course during the ups and downs of their initial implementation. If you can support them through the change, it can make them motivated to keep trying the new ideas.

Let's see how this process works in the scenario involving Ms. Juarez and Michelle.

> As Ms. Juarez shadowed Michelle and visited her classes, she noticed that Michelle seemed agitated and anxious during the beginning of each class. When Michelle first arrived in her classes, she continually looked over toward the doorway, almost appearing to be expecting someone to burst into the room. After about five minutes (when the classroom bustle settled down), Michelle focused on the teacher and the lesson.
>
> Ms. Juarez wanted to know if there were any patterns associated with her disruptions and being asked to leave classes. She went back and looked at her records to see when Michelle was getting into trouble. Sure enough, at least 75 percent of the time that Michelle had been sent to the office occurred at the beginning of a class period. The data confirmed Ms. Juarez's thoughts: Michelle was getting disruptive while she was trying to settle into class.
>
> As a part of her study of Michelle's behaviors, Ms. Juarez also reflected on some of the comments Michelle has made to her when she first arrived in the office after being asked to leave class. Ms. Juarez remembered that Michelle told her about incidents in her home when others (her mom's boyfriend, other relatives, neighbors, and so on) burst into their house and caused conflicts. Many of these situations had resulted in physical altercations that Michelle said upset her. These could be traumatic events for Michelle.
>
> Ms. Juarez called a follow-up meeting with the teachers to share the patterns of behavior she has observed in Michelle. After sharing the data, Ms. Juarez led the group to develop a plan for Michelle to get settled before asking her to focus on the lesson. Everyone agreed to let Michelle get comfortable before asking her to get involved in the lesson. With an initial plan developed, Ms. Juarez knew it would be important to talk with Michelle and explain the plan to her. Since Ms. Juarez had developed a relationship with Michelle, she decided that she should meet with her and explain the plan.

In this scenario, Ms. Juarez was able to use the data she gathered to help the teachers *see* the problem. Once everyone was aware of the pattern of the behaviors, they were motivated to work with Ms. Juarez to develop a plan to address the issues. Developing a plan is just the first step in addressing the problem. Ms. Juarez knows there will be ups and downs and she will need to provide continued follow-up and support for both the teachers and Michelle in order for the plan to be successful. As the teachers implemented the strategy of letting Michelle get settled in before asking her to participate, they saw an improvement in her behaviors.

As school leaders, you can provide an important service to teachers by being able to step back and observe patterns. Because you aren't in the classroom every day, you can provide objective and helpful ideas by connecting the dots related to interactions with trauma-impacted students. This ability is particularly helpful for teachers to recognize and change learning environments that may be contributing to trauma.

Asking teachers to complete an assessment of their learning environment, looking for structures or processes that might be contributing to trauma or adding to traumatic situations, is a key process you should consider. The assessment template in figure 3.1 (page 60) can help teachers identify potential problem areas and make necessary adjustments to make their learning environment more trauma sensitive.

In their article, "Trauma-Informed Leadership in Schools: From the Inside-Out," Nealy-Oparah and Scruggs-Hussein (2018) identify what they call the *eight Rs* or areas of focus for schools and classrooms to become more trauma sensitive. These elements are helpful for you to work on with teachers to reflect about how to make their classrooms and instruction more trauma sensitive.

The first four Rs are focused on teacher behaviors and attitudes. They are all related to teacher responses.

- **Realize:** Trying to understand the situations that some of the students are experiencing

- **Recognize:** Being observant so you can see the signs of trauma and the triggers of student responses to trauma

- **Respond:** Responding in a productive manner to students' reactions to impacts of trauma

- **Resist:** Resisting judgmental responses to trauma-related student behaviors

List the suspected trauma areas that may be impacting your students.

_____

_____

_____

_____

List the processes or procedures in your learning environment that seem to trigger undesirable behaviors.

_____

_____

_____

_____

List the evidence that makes you think these processes or procedures are triggering problems.

_____

_____

_____

_____

Implement changes in processes or procedures that you think would help make your learning environment more trauma sensitive.

_____

_____

_____

_____

What is your timeline for making these changes in your classroom? What resources will you need in order to make these changes?

_____

_____

_____

_____

Source: Eller & Hierck, 2021, p. 56.

Figure 3.1: Assessment for identifying and changing potential learning environment problem areas.

*Visit **go.SolutionTree.com/leadership** for a free reproducible version of this figure.*

The second four Rs are focused on classroom practices and structures that can help mediate the impacts or responses to trauma.

- **Routines:** Having friendly and consistent processes in place for learning, management, and student behavior

- **Rituals:** Designing processes, ceremonies, and celebrations to help students feel valued and special

- **Relationships:** Developing and nurturing positive relationships with students in the school and classroom

- **Regulation:** Providing processes and strategies to help students productively cope with, de-escalate, or let go of the emotions associated with the trauma or traumatic situations they are experiencing so these emotions don't negatively impact their learning experience

As a leader, you can make these eight Rs topics of discussion in collaborative team meetings, in general faculty meetings, or as a part of the conversations related to the teacher evaluation process or other venues that help teachers look beyond their own needs toward their students' needs.

The strategies in other chapters of this book are grounded in these elements. This model could be a good way for you to organize your school priorities and help teachers keep track of their implementation efforts.

As a leader of a trauma-sensitive school, it's important that you also implement and model some of the strategies you are asking teachers to use in their classrooms. Let's see how Principal Allaway does this in leading his school.

> *Principal Allaway knows that he should utilize some of the processes and structures he is asking his teachers to use in their classrooms. By modeling these strategies, he will help them experience and practice them.*
>
> *He starts by redesigning how he operates his faculty meetings. Each meeting starts with relaxing music playing as the teachers enter the room. He changes the normal seating pattern by randomly assigning small-group membership. As the teachers enter the room, they pick up a handout that contains their table assignment. During the meeting, Principal Allaway has teachers up and moving around. This happens as a result of several interactive activities. The old "sit and get" is replaced with small-group interactions. For example, he has*

*small groups share their ideas written on chart paper using a strat-
egy called* carousel brainstorming.

*The movement and interactive activities are not done in a frivolous
manner; Principal Allaway shares the rationale for each activity so
the teachers know why they are doing them. He also asks the small
groups to discuss how they might implement some of these strategies in their classrooms. Staff members consistently report that
faculty meetings have changed from dreaded experiences to valuable times for faculty to interact, collaborate, and develop strategies they can use in their classrooms.*

In the various scenarios presented in this chapter, Principal Allaway purposefully
supports the implementation of structures and processes to help teachers become
more trauma sensitive. While the implementation is not perfect, his support and
leadership are essential to the success of his teachers.

Conclusion

In this chapter, we examined several aspects of leading teachers on the trauma-
sensitive journey. It began with a focus on classroom culture and ended with strategies for structures and processes needed for classroom and whole-school success.

In chapter 4, we focus on the importance of working productively and positively
with the significant adults in the lives of trauma-impacted students. By building
relationships with families, you can help your teachers more easily understand, support, and partner with them. Positive and productive parent-family relationships
help you and your staff provide the supports needed to increase the success of all
students, but especially trauma-impacted students.

QUESTIONS FOR *Reflection*

As you think about what you learned in this chapter and how it can be implemented in your school, reflect on the following questions.

○   How do the individual classroom cultures work together to build the
    whole-school culture? How can you reinforce classroom cultures to build
    a trauma-sensitive school culture?

○ Why is periodic movement critical for trauma-impacted students? Why is it important for teachers to build periodic movement into their classroom lessons and activities?

○ What are the eight Rs discussed in this chapter? How do they help build a trauma-sensitive school culture?

chapter four

Building Relationships
With Parents and Families

Matthew, a sixth-grade student, exhibits impulsive behaviors (like clicking his pen repeatedly or tapping his pencil on his desk) in most of his classes at Benjamin Franklin Middle School. Principal Sawyer often has to remove Matthew from classrooms when his impulsive behaviors disrupt the class. In past years, someone called Matthew's parents whenever there was an issue. The parents responded by telling the caller that there's nothing they can do from home to help with Matthew's behavior at school. There just seemed to be an endless cycle related to Matthew's behavior issues.

This year, Principal Sawyer decides to try a new path. She thinks Matthew must be causing similar issues at home and that his parents may be challenged to deal with them there. She decides that rather than just asking them to deal with Matthew when outbursts or impulsive behaviors occur, it would be better to develop a partnership or relationship with them to work together to help Matthew be successful.

Most parents want their children to succeed. Sometimes, they don't know the best way to help make that happen. After all, when we have children, we don't get an instruction booklet or much outside support. We tackle most issues by ourselves.

In schools, we operate somewhat separately from parents in working with their children. We don't know what the parents have to deal with or how they work with their children at home. We do have training and experience in strategies and methods to work with children, but we may be missing the context or inside knowledge we need to be successful.

Rather than operating as independent entities, the best thing we can do is find ways to build relationships (partnerships) with parents. This chapter offers strategies to build meaningful and helpful relationships with students' parents and families.

This chapter focuses on building relationships with families of students experiencing trauma. It also examines the role that the community can play as you become a trauma-sensitive school. As you read this chapter, focus on the following ideas.

- The importance of building relationships with families of students in trauma

- Strategies for building positive, nonjudgmental relationships with families

- Techniques for building on foundational elements of relationships and positively impacting students' lives

- The unique role of leaders in reaching out to parents and families to help understand and support your trauma-sensitive efforts

The Importance of Building Relationships With Parents and Families

There is widespread debate in education about what constitutes the most accurate predictor of academic achievement. The reality is that it's not socioeconomic status nor how prestigious the school that a child attends. According to the National Parent Teacher Association (2000), "The best predictor of student success is the extent to which families encourage learning at home and involve themselves in their child's education" (p. 1). Helping parents feel comfortable engaging at home and working in collaboration with school requires a strong relationship. Let's look at this aspect of relationships.

After an analysis of numerous studies on parental engagement, educational researchers Nancy E. Hill and Diana F. Tyson (2009) conclude that there is a connection between family involvement and academic achievement. The sooner educators establish parent engagement, the more effective they are in increasing student performance. Not surprisingly, Eric Dearing, Holly Kreider, Sandra Simpkins, and Heather B. Weiss (2006) suggest that parent partnerships formed during elementary school years build a strong foundation for student success and future engagement opportunities. The earlier they engage, and the more committed parents remain, the better the outcomes for *all* students.

Building strong relationships with the families of trauma-impacted students can help these students see teachers are adults they can trust in their lives. As a school leader, you can work together with your faculty to develop a consistent state of engagement. This objective must be the focus of everyone in the school.

Families as Partners for Success

"Two-way communication between parents and teachers [in engaged relationships] commits students to daily attendance and raises class participation levels" (Waterford.org, 2018), while also giving parents the sense of being members of the school community. Tom's personal experience in school leadership validates this fact as he led a school that went from the proverbial rock bottom (and undesirable to potential educators and families) to a school of impact (with educators and parents transferring in due to its success). The single biggest change that took place in the first year was to welcome parents as partners in every aspect of the school's operation. This meant accepting parents as true partners in the school. The school invited families to be part of every committee, including policy, budget, and curriculum, for example. They had the freedom to create structures (such as a quarterly awards ceremony) and provide input. The school invited them to be part of the solution and not just identify concerns. Having parents as advocates during critical times in the life of a school proved invaluable.

This model of communication and authentic engagement means that leaders also benefit. Authentically engaged parents tend to think more highly of educators, which can lead to improved morale. Knowing more about a student's family life can also help teachers with adding content to their lessons to better fit that student's needs or interact more efficiently with families. Research from Anne T. Henderson and Nancy Berla (1994) suggests that classrooms with engaged parents perform better as a whole. As educators with decades of experience, we believe that the larger the team supporting student success, the greater the likelihood of success being achieved.

In developing a positive relationship with parents of students in trauma, it's important for leaders to think about how to gently approach parents and build the relationship in steps. Think of scaffolding the relationship to establish a foundation of comfort, and then build on that foundation.

Students in every classroom come from different backgrounds and home situations. As leaders, it's important to understand and support the varying needs of families and the trauma they are experiencing. According to the National Child Traumatic Stress Network (n.d.):

> All families experience trauma differently. Some factors, such as a child's age or the family's culture or ethnicity, may influence how the family copes and recovers from a traumatic event. Trauma changes families as they work to survive and adapt to their circumstances and environment. While this adjustment may be smooth for some, for others the stress and burden cause them to feel alone, overwhelmed, and less able to maintain vital family functions.

As school leaders, it is imperative that you find ways to reach out to your families, support their needs, and make them aware of the resources they can access in their community. It's a reminder to all families that schools are the hub of the community and that leaders treat that with great responsibility and appreciate the opportunity to have a positive impact.

As the National Child Traumatic Stress Network (2011) suggests, it is important that schools are aware of the impact of trauma on family relationships and functioning. School leaders should work to help members of their school community access supports and treatments that focus on all family members and work to stabilize the whole family unit. The National Child Traumatic Stress Network (2011) emphasizes that schools should look for options that:

- Promote safety for all family members and prevent exposure to further traumas

- Optimize the strengths of the family's cultural or ethnic background, religious or spiritual affiliation, and beliefs to support recovery

- Link families to essential community resources

- Educate families on the signs of posttraumatic stress and how it can affect the family

- Include family-sensitive trauma assessments and evidence-based treatments that actively engage family members

- Help family members talk together about their traumatic experiences and how they were impacted

Every school leader knows the challenges associated with trying to contact families. This becomes increasingly more challenging as the needs of the student become more pronounced. Often, the parents and families you need to spend the most time with have the most infrequent contact with the school. One of the positive things that emerged from the COVID-19 pandemic was an increased connection with students' families. Whether this was born out of school occurring in an entirely different fashion (remote or hybrid learning), the need to establish who was going to enroll in school when face-to-face instruction was put on hold, or simply reporting student progress in a different fashion, there was more communication than schools had previously recorded. The challenge is to keep this going when there isn't a worldwide event driving the need. Making positive contacts with all parents and families should be a priority. Recognizing some of the underlying reasons why some families don't want contact is equally important. As Juliet Vogel and the Family Systems Collaborative Group (2017) state:

> Family resilience will vary depending on several factors: the challenges from the current stressors, the level of pre-existing stress and everyday hassles, the family's coping skills, and the resources available from family members as well as other sources such as the community. (p. 1)

A Foundation of Trust and Support

In *Thriving as a New Teacher*, Eller and Eller (2016) discuss the importance of developing relationships with families. When working with families of students who are experiencing trauma, these relationships are even more crucial than with families who are not experiencing trauma since they benefit from your understanding and support.

In our own experiences living in trauma, our families did not naturally trust authority figures such as teachers. These authority figures could report our families and the situations going on in our homes to law enforcement and social services, who could take action to penalize them. Our families had a natural inclination to cover up or hide the situations. They made overt attempts to present everything as normal whenever someone came around or asked questions.

Just as our own families did, other families in trauma often have the same fear of being judged (and suffering consequences) for the situations they experience and cause with their children. Because of the families' natural mistrust, it's important for leaders to reach out on behalf of the school and try to build trusting relationships with families in trauma. These initial relationships need to be built on nonjudgmental and trusting actions. The first steps toward relationship building may even need to occur on neutral territory, at a site in your community away from both the school building and the home.

Avoid Judgment

It may be tempting to look at other people's situations through your lens and pass judgment. Leaders also may feel the need to support their faculty members and share a perspective that may be inaccurate or unwarranted in the given situation. Withholding judgment is important in working with all parents but especially important when working with parents and families of trauma-impacted students. While they might need help, support, or advice to move forward, your ideas and possibly even your support may fall on deaf ears unless you've developed a trusting relationship with them.

While building relationships with families in trauma can be challenging (because of a variety of factors, including their interest in keeping their struggles private, their own poor school experiences, and so on), the rewards are great. In many cases, these families may have an aversion to working with public officials. Their past experiences with teachers or the principal may have been one where they were judged.

Accepting people as they are can be hard to do, especially in the midst of conflict. However, you'll be able to make a larger impact than if you get oppositional or make suggestions too early in the relationship. As the leader of a team and the de facto figurehead of the school, there is considerable weight to your views and your opinions. Being sensitive to both the situation in your school and the impact of trauma in the lives of your students is a tough balancing act and one that requires leaders to suspend judgment. *We are not suggesting that you ignore dangerous or potentially life-threatening situations.* In most places, educators are all mandatory reporters for abusive and dangerous situations. In these cases, developing a relationship comes second to protecting a child. In most jurisdictions, there is a statutory requirement to report any sign of abuse or disclosure that indicates abuse. There is no leeway nor consideration of fracturing a relationship with the family. It is a legal requirement.

Becoming a healing organization that aims to reduce the impact of trauma means supporting parents, children, and families absent of judgment. Remember to minimize judgment and maximize parents' comfort to help you develop positive working relationships.

Listen First, Talk Later

In verbal communications, it pays to listen more than to speak, especially in the early stages of building a relationship. Using skills such as active listening and paraphrasing can help build trust in a relationship. Putting your own thoughts and ideas on hold and truly listening to what the parents have to say go a long way to building relationships and engagement. Listen at least twice as much as you speak.

Control Negative Reactions

When working with families experiencing trauma, you may learn some information that will surprise or shock you. When hearing news of this nature, your reactions and facial expressions can communicate judgment. Since nonverbal communication makes up much of the message in a conversation, minimizing your nonverbal reactions will make it appear that you are not judging but simply gathering information to assist. When talking with parents, try to control your reactions to surprising news. Framing your thoughts in advance and reminding yourself to watch your reactions can help you to avoid looking surprised or shocked and assist with building necessary bridges.

Focus on the Child

Parents will be more motivated to build a relationship with you if you are able to keep the focus on doing what's best for their children. The fear of judgment about them as people and parents may result in unnecessary suspicion. You'll want to frame your actions around the needs of their child. When parents know that their child's support and success is your first priority, they are much more willing to engage in a relationship. This does not mean that you are not supporting your faculty member, but it does mean that you are seeking solutions motivated by the needs of the student.

Understand Personal Challenging Educational Experiences

Parents whose personal school experiences were marked by little or no success can be intimidated by the school system and might believe they have little or nothing to contribute to their child's education. Some parents of trauma-impacted students may have experienced trauma themselves and may have had poor school experiences. They may feel their voice is of little consequence and may feel out of place attending meetings with other parents. By reaching out to parents or families, you help them see that what you are offering is different than the experiences they had when they were in school. In trying to build a supportive relationship, leaders may have to step outside the normal course of operations and meet parents off campus if the school site itself is a major barrier to this outcome.

Be Aware of Family Cultures

The Michigan Department of Education (2015) notes that "in many countries and cultures, it is accepted that the teacher's responsibility is to educate a student while he or she is at school; the parent is then responsible for education at home" (p. 77). This may lead some immigrant families to show their respect for schools and educators by keeping their distance. Schools need to be diligent about breaking through this barrier. Parents may feel uncomfortable or unwelcome in their child's school if there is a lack of cultural awareness and diversity that they can relate to.

Ensure that your school is welcoming and family friendly—whatever a student's particular family may look like. Post signs in multiple languages that are reflective of your population, and decorate your room and adjoining hallways with works of art and flags of countries represented in your community. Attend cultural events, as parents and community members enjoy seeing educators outside the school setting involved in the community. The American Psychological Association (2003) also offers some guidelines on multicultural education and training.

As the demographics of the typical student in schools change across the United States (see figure 4.1), so too should schools be aware that parents' backgrounds might influence their view toward school and their role within it.

It's important that schools provide parents with the opportunity to view school in a positive light. Actively listening to parents' questions and concerns, and treating these concerns seriously rather than explaining them away, indicates to parents they are part of the team working to ensure success for all students. If background

According to the National Center for Education Statistics (2018), the projected 50.8 million U.S. public school students entering prekindergarten through grade 12 in fall 2020 are expected to include:

- 23.4 million White students
- 14.0 million Hispanic students
- 7.6 million Black students
- 2.8 million Asian students
- 2.3 million students of two or more races
- 0.5 million American Indian/Alaska Native students
- 0.2 million Pacific Islander students

Source: National Center for Education Statistics, 2018.

Figure 4.1: Changing student and family demographics.

experiences include traumatic events, the parent may become a resource for others, or may benefit from the support the school puts in place.

Understand Parent Education Levels

When attempting to build relationships with parents, pay attention to their education levels. Parents of students in trauma may not have graduated from high school as a result of their own traumatic experiences. Parents with education levels lower than yours may feel intimidated in talking with you or could even be resentful of your education level. Try to relate to them as people and be careful not to let your education level get in the way of developing a sound relationship.

Avoid Educational Jargon or Codes

Educators often use jargon with which parents may be unfamiliar. This jargon or code is clear to educators but not to parents. The jargon in a conversation may sound like this: "Hello, Mr. Smith. Our guiding coalition met as a PLC to look at our latest CFA, and we are proposing that your child receive additional Tier 2 RTI support." This insider's code inhibits the ability of parents to understand and engage in their child's education. It may also work counter to any steps previously mentioned and send the unintentional message that this principal wants to keep parents at a distance. When working with parents, be sure to always define any terms as well as their significance for their student. Being clear and simple can go a long way in helping you develop a good relationship with parents.

Focus on Family Needs

Focus on family needs to provide a foundation for your relationship efforts. If you strive to build relationships based on what's good or helpful for *them*, you'll have more success. How can you determine parent or family needs? Do a survey of parents to gauge their interest in learning more about your school, school policies, parenting skills, or child development. Then work with them to develop parent education programs based on your survey results. This may help families fully engage in their child's education. These opportunities could focus on academic topics like understanding report cards and assessments, parent-teacher conferences, and home support, or family-related topics such as child development, discipline, or community support services (Michigan Department of Education, 2015). One strategy we used as leaders was coffee and conversation, which was a regularly scheduled time when parents could drop in and share thoughts, ask questions, provide advice, and let the principal know a little about themselves. This became a source of information for various activities and events held in the school throughout the year as the families were willing to assist, if needed.

Trauma can alter the way a student sees the world, making it suddenly seem a much more dangerous and frightening place. Students may find it more difficult to trust both their environment and the people in it and may need help to rebuild a sense of safety and security. As a leader, make a point to share some strategies with parents and families (through emails, newsletters, the school website, and so on) that can assist their children dealing with trauma, such as the following.

- Establish a predictable structure and schedule to increase stability.

- Make sure their child has space and time for rest, play, and fun.

- Speak of the future and make plans to help counteract the common feeling among trauma-impacted children that the future is scary, bleak, and unpredictable.

- Reassure their child and help place the situation in context, as children often personalize situations and worry about their own safety even if the traumatic event occurred far away (Smith, Robinson, & Segal, 2021).

- Manage their own stress, remaining calm, relaxed, and focused in an effort to help their child manage theirs.

Be Aware of Parent and Family Roles and Perceptions

As previously mentioned, as the demographics of the typical school student change across the United States, schools should be aware that some students' parents have backgrounds that might influence their view toward school and their role within it. Some immigrant families might keep their distance from the school and educators as a sign of respect, not disinterest. Schools and educators need to be diligent about understanding the various perspectives that arise out of different cultures and breaking through these barriers to inform and educate families about the need for their support.

Let's see how Principal Sawyer, from a previous scenario, handles the school's relationship with Matthew's family.

> *Principal Sawyer sees the need to develop a relationship (partnership) with Matthew's parents to work together to improve his behavior. She understands that in order for this relationship to work, she needs to approach the parents in a nonjudgmental manner. She also knows that it would be better to meet with them on their turf rather than at the school.*
>
> *Instead of simply calling the parents in response to Matthew's behavior issues, Principal Sawyer decides to walk Matthew home, since he only lives a couple of blocks away, and talk with his parents. She calls them to let them know there was a problem at school and that she's bringing Matthew home.*
>
> *Principal Sawyer walks Matthew home and asks him to go inside and get one of his parents. When Matthew's dad comes to the door, Principal Sawyer shares the details of the incident at school. Matthew's dad turns to Matthew and asks him about the incident. Matthew confirms what happened. Principal Sawyer then tells Matthew's father what she is planning to do to help Matthew to get his behavior under control. She walks with Matthew back to school, and they start to develop a plan.*

In this scenario, Principal Sawyer's decision to walk Matthew home may sound bold or harsh, but it's effective because his parents see that she is interested (and serious) in helping Matthew get his behavior on track. In future situations, Principal Sawyer (and even some of the teachers) meets the parents off-site to develop plans and ideas to help Matthew be successful. Because of the outreach, Matthew's parents know that Principal Sawyer and the teachers are interested in being personally involved and invested in Matthew's success.

Use a Variety of Communication Methods

Traditionally, schools have been able to build relationships with students and families through face-to-face or verbal methods. In the modern, technological world, they may need to use other methods. According to a Blackboard (2016) paper "Trends in Community Engagement: How K–12 Schools Are Meeting the Expectations of Parents for Digital Communications," there is an emerging form of communication to which some schools have been slow to respond. Blackboard (2016) also reveals that:

- 87 percent of parents indicated this year that a personal email was the most effective vehicle for communicating with them, an increase of 36 percent since 2010.

- 55 percent of parents would like their child's teacher or school to simply "text them" when they want to communicate information. In 2010, text messaging was the preference of only five percent of parents.

- Only 50 percent of the parents noted that a face-to-face meeting was the most effective way to communicate information to them, a significant decrease from just one year ago when 64 percent of parents valued the type of communications approach.

- Only 48 percent of parents chose a personal phone call as the most effective way to communicate information to them.

- Parents of elementary students who are under 40 years of age themselves are the most supportive of the use of emerging digital tools to support school-to-home communications.

As we all saw during the COVID-19 pandemic and resulting remote learning, parents still needed communication links to their child's school (Schwartz, Grant, Diliberti, Hunter, & Setodji, 2020). Anecdotally, the authors heard in many schools about the increase in parent communication that occurred as a result of using the available technology. *Zoom* became a common word used in most U.S. households. Don't take this to mean that schools abandoned all other forms of communication, including many of the traditional methods. It does indicate that educators need to explore additional options on the road to engaging parents in ways that suit them and are accessible. While exploring every option to ensure parents become fully engaged in their child's education, it's also important to recognize that sometimes there are additional challenges that may work against your best efforts, such as access to the internet or electronic devices.

Parent and Family Engagement

So far, we've outlined the importance of building relationships with parents and families of trauma-impacted students. Once a foundational relationship has been formed, you can move forward to develop a more collaborative relationship—parent engagement.

You can think of parent engagement as parents and the school sharing a responsibility to help their children learn and meet educational goals. Even though we have been focusing on developing relationships with parents of students experiencing trauma, you'll want to develop relationships with *all* your students' parents.

Parent engagement in education matters now more than ever for all students, but is especially important for trauma-impacted students. Educational inequity has existed long before the COVID-19 pandemic began to impact schools. However, the sudden transition to distance learning shone a light on the huge gap between those who had access to technology and could function in a remote environment with limited adult support and those who did not.

Research from Blackboard (2016) heightens this concern, showing a decline in parents who believe face-to-face, intimate parent-teacher communication is effective. Waterford.org (2018) states, "Parents now prefer remote methods of communication, like online student portals, and they are less likely to attend parent-teacher conferences or school activities." This should raise a red flag for schools as to what it means for parent engagement. Families in trauma may have fewer resources and less ability to communicate via email or even over the phone. You need to look at ways to reach out to these parents and families in ways that work for them.

Factors Impacting Parent and Family Engagement

A myriad of factors can inhibit the capacity for parents to become engaged with their child's school. Leading the list is the change in economic pressures affecting most families. These same economic pressures can contribute to childhood trauma. It is a significant challenge to make ends meet with only one income to pay the bills. In homes where both adults are working, this leaves precious little time at the end of the day to engage with schools. Getting dinner on the table and having a bit of quality time supersede attending a school event. Other parents have scheduling or transportation issues that make volunteering or attending parent-teacher conferences tough.

It's critical that schools reach out early and often to build these connections with parents. If this parent-teacher relationship isn't established early in the year, parents may feel they are not welcome at school. When you engage them early and hopefully before a major problem occurs, then at the first indication of a concern, they can help solve the problem before it becomes a full-blown issue.

You must also recognize the challenges can become more prevalent for some groups. Research from Child Trends (2018) suggests that parent involvement is lowest in families below the poverty line, families with older children, families where the parents do not speak the area's primary language, and families with parents who did not graduate high school. Our own anecdotal evidence is a reminder that a lack of parental success in school is often a precursor to a lack of parental involvement in school (Sheldon & Jung, 2015). We discussed the importance of these issues earlier, but it's good to keep them in the forefront as we work to build family relationships.

Family Help With Aggressive Behavior

Childhood trauma can prompt many reactions in children at school. One of these can be aggressive behavior. Aggressive behavior is a common area for which schools can reach out to parents and families for help. In addition to stopping a behavior that is harmful to the students and others in the classroom, addressing this issue with parents and families is crucial for future success.

Research suggests that when students experience a supporting and caring school environment, and their parents are engaged with their school, they are less likely to become involved in substance abuse, violence, and other problem behaviors (Hawkins, Catalano, Kosterman, Abbott, & Hill, 1999), including behaviors associated with HIV and STD risk (Van Tieu & Koblin, 2009).

As you review the strategies in the following section, think about how you can customize some of them to match the strengths of the parents you wish to engage in your school.

How to Increase Parent and Family Engagement

While we often hear that parents tend to be more involved in their children's school during the elementary years, we maintain it's never too late to build the foundations for parent-teacher communication in school. Students in trauma benefit tremendously when parents are engaged in their learning. Clearly, as with most successful school endeavors, the sooner you reach out, the more equipped your students will be to reach their academic potential and be more supported by their family as they do so. Tom's eleven years of experience as an administrator of a grades 7–9 middle school also reinforced how powerful a force the parents became and how significant they were, not only in the lives of their children but in the life of the school.

Try these parent and family engagement strategies to transform involvement into meaningful parent and family partnerships. These strategies will carry more weight if you, as a leader, model and deliver these expectations and encourage teachers to do the same.

- Reach out to parents at the beginning of the school year, and share your contact information. By talking with and getting to know parents before your team actually works with their children, you'll be better able to listen and gather their perspectives. Reaching out early helps you develop relationships before you encounter difficulties. Tom had a regular coffee and conversation opportunity for parents beginning every school year.

- With parents of trauma-impacted students, you may need to reach out in more personal ways. For example, having personal conversations with parents at the start of the year goes a long way in building successful relationships. That way, when parents have questions or concerns, they'll feel comfortable reaching out.

- Provide opportunities for parents and families to connect with the school. Various forums to engage parents and families include volunteer shifts, class activities, or parent-leadership committees where they define your school's purpose or have input in the budget planning.

- Share your school goals or expectations openly with parents, and ask them to do the same. Let them know what happens when occasional poor judgment from their children occurs.

- Connect with parents on a face-to-face basis as much as possible. In addition to personal communication, use emails, texts, or apps to keep parents up to date on upcoming school or district events, and assist (if needed) in creating a parent section in your methods of communication, for example, a column in the school bulletin or space on the school Facebook page.

- Support initiatives presented by parents that support the work of the school community. For instance, Tom had parents who created their own quarterly system of recognition for students based on their efforts, aligning with the purpose of the school.

Address common challenges that inhibit or prevent parent and family engagement like scheduling conflicts with parents' jobs or activities, or an intimidating atmosphere. As the opening of this chapter indicates, parents may have had past negative experiences with school, so they may not easily recognize the positive experiences you and your team are trying to create. Meet parents where they need you to meet them and build from there.

The Centers for Disease Control and Prevention (2012) proposes a framework for schools to consider when they are looking to increase parent and family engagement in schools.

1. **Connect** with parents by building a positive relationship and communicating the school's vision to work together with parents to guide children's health and learning.

2. **Engage** parents by providing a variety of activities and frequent occasions to fully involve parents including providing parenting support, increasing communication with parents, creating volunteer opportunities, supporting learning at home, encouraging parents to be part of decision making in schools and collaborating with the community.

3. **Sustain** parent engagement by addressing the common challenges to getting and keeping parents engaged such as scheduling conflicts, transportation, making parents feel welcome in the school and supporting teachers in building relationships with families. (American Psychological Association, 2014a)

The CDC (2012) goes on to state that parent engagement in schools is a shared responsibility in which schools commit to reaching out to engage parents in meaningful ways, and parents commit to actively supporting their children's learning and development. This support improves children's learning, development, and health.

Parent Engagement With Helping Their Trauma-Impacted Child

Earlier in this chapter, we shared that in order to build a relationship with parents of students experiencing trauma, it is important to avoid judgment and providing advice. We made this recommendation because in many cases, the trauma the student is experiencing is caused by some behavior of the parent or someone else in the home. If we jump to judgment too quickly, the parent may put up a wall and withdraw from the relationship. If this happens, the behavior will go underground, and you will not be able to make a difference in the child's life.

We are *not* saying that, in order to develop a relationship with a parent, you should ignore issues of abuse or neglect caused by the parent. When you see signs of abuse or neglect, you need to report those in compliance with the laws of your state or province.

Once you determine that the parents or family are not causing the trauma, you can develop a trusting relationship with them and gradually start to work with them to help their child develop resilience. You may need to move very slowly to maintain the trust while helping the student deal with the traumatic situation. Your relationship with students' families may not develop in the same manner. You may not be able to find projects for some students to do after school to reduce the time they are alone at home, but by working with the parent or guardian, you can develop a level of trust to the point where you can find ways to collaborate with them in the best interest of their children.

One important aspect of support is helping parents and families build resilience. Leaders might view family resilience as the maintenance or restoration of the family's balance between expectations and the coping strategies available to them. Vogel and the Family Systems Collaborative Group (2017) suggests leaders can support resilience with interventions that help families to:

- Reduce the number and intensity of stressors.
- Increase/improve their coping strategies.

- Increase access to resources.

- Reappraise the situation and adjust expectations of the situation and/or themselves. (p. 5)

Throughout this journey, leaders should expect some stumbles, and possibly regression in some skills, before they achieve resilience. If you are willing to accept that acquiring these skills might be a challenge for your highly skilled, professional educators, you should expect no less for parents who may or may not possess comparable skills.

Let's see how the partnership between Matthew's parents and Benjamin Franklin Middle School has evolved over time.

> As a result of continued clear and direct communication, Principal Sawyer and Matthew's parents have formed a partnership. Matthew's parents are straightforward and direct when issues arise, as is Principal Sawyer. Because of this direct communication, they have developed a sense of respect for each other. Throughout their growing relationship, they have shared ideas and strategies that have worked to help calm Matthew. Principal Sawyer has learned ideas from Matthew's parents, and she has been able to share ideas with them. Over time, both parties have worked together to help Matthew stay relaxed and focused. They are both interested in Matthew's success.

In this scenario, the development of basic communication, then working to understand each other, and finally the development of a partnership is beneficial to the success of the student. Parents of trauma-impacted students may be experiencing trauma themselves and reluctant to share their situations with you as the principal. If you seek to get to know them in a nonjudgmental way, you may be able to understand and communicate with them. It's definitely a goal worth working toward.

Community Connections and Support

Thinking back to our own teacher training and the beginning of our careers, we recall that we did not possess the requisite skills to offer much more than a receptive ear and a willingness to support a student and his or her family. While this is important, it's equally important to recognize there are people who have trained many years to be able to offer some of the mental health support that could be beyond what educators trained for. Leaders must become aware of the services their community offers and how to access those services. While we suggest that much more training is needed for all educators to become trauma sensitive, we also know that we'll need some expertise that exists beyond the walls of the school. Schools should create links to mental health consultation and services for staff, students, and families.

Maura McInerney and Amy McKlindon (2014) suggest it might look like this:

- For staff, clinical supports include the opportunity to participate in sessions with their peers and a clinician to confidentially discuss specific cases, reflect on experiences of secondary trauma, and learn and practice strategies for working with children and families.

- For students and families, school staff should refer families to appropriate mental health resources and following up on referrals. Trusting relationships between parents/caregivers, school staff, and mental health providers can help ensure success. (p. 8)

We know that community and cultural context can influence a family's response to trauma and stress. Vogel and the Family Systems Collaborative Group (2017) state, "Community-wide stressors such as poverty or community violence add to family stress. Community supports—both formal programs and informal social supports—can foster resilience" (p. 1). A family's beliefs, and ultimately their ability to cope with adversity, are impacted by their cultural and social norms that have been ingrained over generations. Leaders who bring the community into their school, devote time to understanding different cultural perspectives, and rely on the expertise of their broader community will find they are not alone on the journey to becoming trauma sensitive.

Conclusion

In this chapter, we examined ideas and strategies to help build positive relationships with parents and families to help trauma-impacted students. In many cases, parents or other family members have had some role in creating the traumatic situation, but in some they have not. Once positive relationships have been established, you can move to the next level to involve and engage the parents or guardians. The strategies we outlined in this chapter are designed to help families of children who have experienced trauma, but you also can use them with all your students' families.

As leaders work to help students and teachers in every classroom work through traumatic situations and build the resilience they need to both survive and thrive, developing partnerships with and engaging parents will be crucial. Relationship building and engagement takes time, but the time you invest in these relationships will benefit students both inside and outside the classroom. This is surely a worthy investment.

In chapter 5, you'll learn ideas and strategies to begin planning your journey toward becoming a trauma-sensitive school. In this journey, you'll be making your school not only better for students impacted by trauma, but better for all learners.

QUESTIONS FOR *Reflection*

As you think about what you learned in this chapter and how it can be implemented in your school, reflect on the following questions.

- Why is developing a relationship so important in working productively with parents? What are some ways you can build relationships with students' parents and families?

- What are some activities you would consider to increase parent and family presence in your school? How can you move from parent-family involvement to parent-family engagement?

- Why would parents who may have a role in the trauma their child is experiencing be reluctant to work with you? How can you build trust while addressing their child's needs?

- What are the specific ideas you have learned in this chapter? How can you implement them in your school and in your work with parents?

- What resources are available in your community that you can access or build partnerships with as you become trauma sensitive?

chapter five

Building the Foundation for a Trauma-Sensitive School

At Grimes Elementary School, the building instructional leadership team has worked with Principal McSmith to analyze the data related to student trauma. Many students come from single-parent families, are absent frequently, are of low socioeconomic status, and experience other factors that may contribute to childhood trauma. In analyzing the data, the building instructional leadership team recommends that the staff implement trauma-sensitive practices to help meet the needs of the students and teachers at Grimes.

The building instructional leadership team decides to act as the guiding coalition for the trauma-sensitive project. They agree to participate in a book study about trauma-sensitive practices. They also agree to work together to implement a series of common procedures to help provide stability for their students. They will implement these common practices for three months and then assess the results.

The building instructional leadership team also decides that there should be some general awareness sessions on trauma and trauma-sensitive practices for the whole staff so everyone has the same basic information. The team schedules a series of mini-sessions for three weeks after school so the staff can learn more about trauma, the original ACEs study, the impact of trauma on the brain, and other foundational aspects of trauma.

By implementing these and other strategies, the building instructional leadership team and Principal McSmith are helping to build a foundation for the success of the trauma-sensitive initiative they will be implementing.

In this scenario, the principal and the building instructional leadership team understand the importance of building the foundation for success in implementing the initiative. By taking the time to build this foundation, they are helping to begin the process of changing the mindset of all the staff toward accepting and embracing the concepts and ideas related to trauma-sensitive instruction. This common understanding and mindset will be important as the implementation moves forward and the staff encounter some of the issues that typically emerge in any change project.

In this chapter, you will learn about the importance of building a strong foundation for the trauma-sensitive initiative you are working to implement. This foundation will help you build the buy-in and common vision to help sustain the implementation, even as it encounters some of the bumps that may get in the way of success and make people want to go back to the old ways of doing business. As you read this chapter, focus on the following:

- The differences between traditional ways and trauma-informed ways of working with students

- The importance of mindset and perspective

- Which practices to keep, modify, or discard when setting the foundation for a trauma-sensitive school

- How to support teams and individuals in understanding the concept of trauma-sensitive instruction and a trauma-sensitive school

These and other strategies will help you as you do the important work of building a foundation for success as you work toward becoming a trauma-sensitive school.

Traditional Versus Trauma Sensitive

When a school moves from traditional methods of dealing with trauma and its impact to a trauma-sensitive model that focuses on reducing the impact of trauma and promoting healing, the change takes a lot of planning. Suppose a student arrives at school in the morning and is greeted positively and appropriately by an adult. The student either ignores the greeting or mumbles something under his breath. In this moment, the adult has a choice to make as to her next action. Traditionally, the adult might have moved immediately to the power position and issued a consequence. There is another way.

One goal of a trauma-sensitive school is to shift perspectives in staff dialogue from "What's wrong with that student?" to "What has happened to that student?"

and "What does he or she need?" When using a trauma lens for student behavior, the focus shifts from attributing misbehavior to the student's personal characteristics to understanding how the student's exposure to toxic stress and trauma impacts his or her development and behavior. Joyce Dorado suggests this trauma lens "provides context . . . fosters compassion, and helps us to see strengths in the face of adversity" (as cited in Adams, 2013).

What does the journey toward becoming a trauma-sensitive school look like? How will you know you and your team are making progress?

The move toward becoming a trauma-sensitive school involves an examination of every aspect of a school's operation to see how each might impact students in a negative manner. This process is not easy, and it's not emphasized in any teacher education program. As educational author and consultant Chris Weber (2018) notes, "Educators were not prepared in our teacher-preparation courses, in most cases, to teach behavioral skills; their training focused on the teaching and learning of academic skills" (p. 128). The lack of preparation for teaching behavioral skills is compounded when teachers face the extremely challenging behaviors that emerge as a result of traumatic experiences. These encounters with trauma-impacted students make it clear that teachers need much more training in this area, and this training must begin at the earliest stages of teacher education.

The necessary tools for becoming trauma sensitive require a collective commitment and desire to grow as a team. The journey will take time; however, the alternative of *not* becoming trauma sensitive is both untenable and unsustainable if schools want to function as places of healing for trauma-impacted students. The role of the leader becomes one of facilitating the conversations, engaging the expertise of outside resources as needed, and modeling the expectations in their own interactions with students and staff. As Weber (2018) states, "Leadership is critical in all school functions that intend to significantly improve student outcomes. Administrators listen, learn, serve, and support" (p. 129). As school leaders become aware of, and sensitive to, the evidence and impact of trauma, they must lead the charge to develop new policies and programs that address the varied needs of *all* learners.

Consider this statement from Dominique Smith, Nancy Frey, Ian Pumpian, and Douglas Fisher (2017) as you contemplate your move from a traditional view of students and their behavior to a more trauma-sensitive approach:

> There is no equity in keeping ourselves unaware and insensitive to the
> huge number of children who should expect their schools to be aware,

sensitive, and responsive to their mental health and well-being. Our failure to do this compromises the very foundation of our educational missions and every other initiative to provide more students the quality educational programs and outcomes we all value. (p. 51)

Finding fault or looking for someone to blame for the current state of affairs at schools is not the point. Educators need to accept where they are and then begin to plan for where they want to be. What growth opportunities (not weaknesses) exist in your school or district? Embrace these opportunities with enthusiasm as the leader of a team committed to moving forward. It may help you to offer the following scenario to your team as a starting point in how a traditional response contrasts with a trauma-sensitive response.

> Greg is a new fifth-grade student to your school, even though school has been in session for two months. Your school is his fourth in the last year, and the likelihood of him completing the year with you is pretty slim. On his first day in class, the teacher approached him at his desk and went to place a hand on Greg's shoulder as a friendly gesture. Greg flinched and pushed the teacher's hand away. The teacher sent him out of the class, but Greg did not leave quietly; instead, he offered a few choice words to the teacher.

Let's look at this scenario from both a traditional and a trauma-sensitive perspective.

- **Traditional response:** The teacher explains to the principal that he was being welcoming, as per school expectations. Greg's response was totally uncalled for and demanded a clear response. The teacher needed to be supported by the office. Physical aggression cannot be tolerated or excused, and this student needed to learn that right away. Immediate and major consequences were expected if only to serve as an example to the rest of the students in the classroom. Greg's disrespect as he was leaving class also needs to be addressed, and it's reasonable to suspend him. He needs to learn that he cannot behave that way in school.

- **Trauma-sensitive response:** While the office is still sensitive to the situation, the teacher and principal discuss it further and wonder if the teacher's action unintentionally created a fear response in Greg. They consider whether Greg's constant moves between schools have left him feeling disconnected and misinterpreting even the slightest of gestures. They understand the response comes from a place of mistrust and is the typical fight response. They realize that putting extra demands or expectations on the student right now will cause further escalation and make the situation worse. Their prime concern is to sort out how to help the student feel safe, so he is able to learn in their classroom. They commit to finding out more about Greg's needs from any resources at their disposal (including colleagues at other schools and in their own school). They also embrace the notion that they may have to teach the desired behaviors rather than simply give Greg negative consequences for the undesirable ones.

It won't be easy for you and your team to move away from the traditional, familiar response, but you need to decide if you are interested in achieving new results and outcomes. To understand and support trauma-impacted students, you need to change your mindset and perspective. Educators must stop seeing these students as willfully acting out to disrupt the classroom or refusing to engage in learning. Instead, they should understand that:

- Students' responses are adaptive patterns based on their personal experiences and are not always aligned with expected school behaviors.

- Students are seeking to meet their needs (remember, behavior is communication).

- Students have difficulty regulating and understanding emotions.

- Students lack important academic and behavioral skills to be successful in school.

- Students' past experiences have led them to believe that adults cannot be trusted.

Educators at trauma-sensitive schools recognize the prevalence and impact of traumatic occurrences in students' lives. They work to create a flexible framework that provides universal supports, is sensitive to the unique needs of students, and is mindful of ensuring students are not impacted by trauma at school.

In summary, an educator with a traditional view might assign Greg's actions to anger management problems that have a myriad of potential causes, such as attention-deficit hyperactivity disorder (ADHD). This person may see Greg as choosing to act out and disrupt class because he is uncontrollable, destructive, or nonresponsive. An educator with a trauma-sensitive view might look for causes for unwanted behaviors, such as Greg seeking to have his needs met, having difficulty self-regulating emotions, or lacking the necessary skills to regulate his emotions. Does he have a negative view of the world ("Adults can't be trusted"), or was his trauma response triggered? In the traditional response, an educator might conclude Greg needs consequences to correct behavior or may need an ADHD evaluation. In the trauma-sensitive response, an educator might conclude that Greg needs to learn skills to regulate his emotions. His teachers, led by school leadership, need to provide support.

Staff Attitudes and Beliefs

As a leader of a school or district, how much training have you received in becoming more trauma sensitive? Ask yourself, "Has your gain in knowledge been driven by personal choice rather than being a requirement of your role?" Then, imagine where most educators are on this important learning curve. How do you think teachers in your school might respond to these three questions?

1. During your preservice teacher training, how much instruction in recognizing childhood trauma did you receive?

2. During your preservice teacher training, how much instruction in supporting students experiencing childhood traumatic stress did you receive?

3. How satisfied or dissatisfied are you with the preservice training you received on supporting students with childhood traumatic stress?

If your first response is to suggest most of your faculty might be on the lower end of a Likert scale for each of the questions, then the focus shifts to this query: "How will you lead the team to becoming a more trauma-sensitive school?" In *Addressing the Epidemic of Trauma in Schools* (National Council of State Education Associations, 2019), the authors note that there is "a critical need for more educator training across the profession to raise awareness and understanding of the impact of trauma on brain development and student behavior" (p. 14). Who might take the lead on such an endeavor? The answer is quite obvious, and the subjects in the study didn't shy away from sharing their thoughts. Participants "underscored the need for a supportive school administration with a commitment to addressing student trauma, behavior issues, and secondary stress among educators" (National Council of State Education Associations, 2019, p. 14). Leadership matters, especially when previous training and exposure might have been minimal.

As a leader, you must consider teacher attitudes and beliefs in understanding classroom practices and conducting teacher professional learning. Equally important is determining what happens in preservice teacher training as to how educators prepare to work with trauma-impacted students. As leaders, principals must consider all these variables when shifting to become more trauma sensitive. As Virginia Richardson (1996) suggests:

> Except for the student teaching element, preservice teacher education seems a weak intervention. It is sandwiched between two powerful forces: previous life history, particularly that related to being a student, and classroom experience as a student teacher and teacher. Experience as a student is important in setting images of teaching that drive initial classroom practice, and experience as a teacher is the only way to develop the practical knowledge that eventually makes routine at least some aspects of classroom practice and provides alternative approaches when faced with dilemmas. (p. 113)

Filling the space between the two powerful influences that Richardson (1996) identifies falls in the bailiwick of the school leader. The participants in the study that formed the basis for *Addressing the Epidemic of Trauma in Schools* emphasized the importance of "including trauma training in teacher preparation programs to stem the high burnout rate among early-career educators" (National Council of State Education Associations, 2019, p. 14) while also recognizing that school and district leaders play a significant role in assigning new teachers to schools and classrooms that may be disproportionately populated by students exhibiting high levels of traumatic stress. Putting teachers with a lack of relevant skills and experience into a situation where they would have a high need for those skills does not seem like an effective plan. Melanie-Anne Atkins and Susan Rodger (2016) note, "Preservice teacher education in mental health and mental health literacy is essential to creating the conditions necessary to support the mental health and wellness of children and youth in schools" (p. 93).

Tashiana Stafford and Tatiana Duchak (2020) identify the following considerations for school leaders as they work with their faculty to build a more trauma-sensitive school:

1. Train all educators, staff, and school personnel in childhood trauma, the signs and symptoms, and its impact on learning and development.

    Consider—

    i. Routine training [of] staff on understanding trauma and its impact on learning and behavior.

    ii. Opportunities for quarterly "refreshers" where staff can revisit previously covered material as well as actively participate in activities to learn specific classroom interventions.

    iii. Making available to staff educational materials regarding recognizing the signs and symptoms of trauma, as well as informational guides, student worksheets, and handouts.

2. Promote connectedness and resiliency within school staff

Consider—

    i. Offering opportunities for educators and school personnel to feel supported and a part of a larger community [through] team-building or community days, appreciation projects, support circles/groups, venues and space to vent frustrations and seek support.

    ii. Provide educators and personnel with the opportunity to correct and learn [from any missteps].

    iii. Promote school-wide connectedness by pairing students with an adult "mentor," and build in opportunities for a student and his or her mentor to develop a meaningful relationship.

3. Prioritize social-emotional learning.

Consider—

    i. Supporting educators as they adjust classroom instruction time to accommodate some emphasis on social emotional learning.

    ii. Review and update school policies, [practices, and procedures] to align with a trauma-informed approach

    iii. Model trauma-informed attitudes, behaviors, and interventions for staff and students. (pp. 18–19)

To this list, we might add trauma training and mental health and wellness education. Keeping in mind the skills and relative capacity of each team member, carefully match each teacher with a classroom requisite to his or her skill level on dealing with trauma. As the work suggested by Stafford and Duchak (2020) becomes more entrenched, and you shift toward becoming a healing (trauma-reducing) site, your team will also be involved in scheduling students to ensure the most productive outcomes. As Atkins and Rodger (2016) indicate, "We can help new or future teachers mitigate the negative effects of professional work demands by raising their awareness of the signs, determinants, and consequences of burnout and the availability of support systems and coping strategies" (p. 108). Leaders lead when the pathway becomes narrow and unlit.

What to Stop, Start, and Continue

As you become more comfortable with understanding the current attitudes and beliefs of your team, the next logical step is to examine the tools they can utilize to analyze both current policy, practice, and procedures and the tools or skills needed to positively impact the move toward becoming a healing organization. An activity that Williams and Hierck (2015) talk about in their best-selling book, *Starting a Movement*, is the Stop-Start-Continue activity. This process is an open, honest, reflective, and collaborative dialogue regarding high-leverage behaviors that help you move toward your desired outcome.

What should you stop, start, and continue doing in order to create your desired outcome? In every school, this question is asked and answered in various forms. The challenge is that they're typically done in forms that don't allow leadership to gather and grow from feedback. In the right environment, staff members will come up with powerful, creative, and productive answers to these questions. By taking an inclusive approach (including everyone in the analysis), leaders create ownership for aligned behaviors and a more targeted list of what needs to change.

While it takes more time to gather team feedback rather than simply decide for them what will start, stop, and continue, involving the team in defining actions increases their ability to manage and accelerate necessary change. When we talk about the shift to aligning behaviors, we mean lasting and fundamental change in the way people do business on a daily basis, not just a cosmetic shift in which people merely pay lip service to a new way of doing things.

Use the template in figure 5.1 (page 94) to work with your team to determine what your school needs to stop, start, and continue to begin the process of becoming a more trauma-sensitive organization.

The conclusion of this activity will lay the groundwork for leaders to take the next step of the journey—identifying, encouraging, and supporting desired strategies and behaviors. As noted previously, the road to becoming a trauma-sensitive (and ultimately a trauma-reducing) school is a long journey. We suggest that schools embarking on this journey recognize that it requires three to five years relative to your starting point. Once the desired result is identified, teams look at current policies, practices, and procedures for alignment with this desired result. What behaviors are engendered by these policies, procedures, and practices? Which of

Desired Result:

Behaviors to STOP:

1	
2	
3	
4	
5	

Behaviors to START:

1	
2	
3	
4	
5	

Behaviors to CONTINUE:

1	
2	
3	
4	
5	

Figure 5.1: Start, stop, and continue activity template.

*Visit **go.SolutionTree.com/leadership** for a free reproducible version of this figure.*

these behaviors are impeding your move toward your goals and should be stopped? This is challenging, particularly if some of those behaviors had positive outcomes in the past. Similarly, what behaviors might your team need to start using with students as you become more trauma aware? There also are most likely some behaviors your team could continue using, possibly (but not always necessarily) with some adjustments.

Building Blocks for the Foundation

A trauma-sensitive approach in schools and districts must involve understanding how trauma affects students. As mentioned previously, this approach encourages adults to respond to students rather than blame them for their behavior. Becoming a trauma-sensitive school is not a checklist, nor should it be viewed as an intervention. The reality, and perhaps biggest challenge when schools adopt this approach, is that the change to educators' understanding when they begin this new approach has no end point. Becoming trauma sensitive is a process—a schoolwide, daily approach that involves understanding and attending to the specific needs of individuals impacted by childhood traumatic experiences. A critical component of all trauma-sensitive approaches is the foundation of strong, trusting, consistent, and predictable relationships between adults and trauma-impacted students.

To be clear, a schoolwide, trauma-sensitive approach requires more than modifying discipline policies and training teachers. As Carmel Hobbs, Dane Paulsen, and Jeff Thomas (2019) suggest, the shift means schools must change the following:

> Both teacher practice and school-wide procedures and policies that pertain to school and classroom structure, providing systemic supports for students across the school, staffing models, communication and connection with families and the community, and overarching philosophical standpoints that understand, respect, and respond to the individual needs of students.

We suggest that schools should have a three-year plan, survey their current reality (you must begin where you are), and start the journey. This starting point will be unique to your school, and leaders must ensure to keep focus on their own school and not other school sites. Comparisons to other schools are rarely based on full or accurate information and serve largely to deflate progress if the community views your school as being "less than" or "farther behind" other schools in your district or elsewhere. The growth that needs to happen at your site, with your team, serves to meet the needs of *your* students and *your* community. It is contextualized even with some overarching general themes.

Tom Brunzell, Lea Waters, and Helen Stokes (2015) identify two major areas of concern where gaps might be prevalent in teacher practice or knowledge regarding trauma-impacted students: (1) dysregulated stress response, and (2) disrupted attachment styles. There are strategies associated with each of these areas that can form the basis of your next step in the journey. Let's examine some strategies to address each gap.

Dysregulated Stress Response

Brunzell, Stokes, and Waters (2016) state, "A student's dysregulated stress response limits their capacity for learning and regulating their behavior because their body is instead reserving energy that would typically be used for learning and concentration" (p. 71). In other words, students are so primed to respond and so ready for a typical adult response that they are distracted from any learning. Two strategies that teachers can employ are to adopt trauma-sensitive classroom management strategies and provide predictable and consistent learning environments.

Adopt Trauma-Sensitive Classroom Management Strategies

Many educators are familiar with the work of B. F. Skinner (1953) who suggests that students' behavior is a result of external factors—those things beyond their control. His work suggests that rewards and punishments can be used in appropriate doses to modify the behavior, resulting in the student becoming less disruptive. However, it's rare that the behavior is motivated by the current classroom conditions and more likely related to factors outside the classroom. Temporarily bribing a student does not lead to a long-term solution. Educators also may be familiar with the work of William Glasser (1999) who advocates a problem-solving approach to negative behavior that involves engaging the student in resolving the problem—the notion that the dignity of the child can be preserved while the problem behavior is resolved.

Becoming trauma sensitive is to commit to taking a proactive rather than reactive approach to discipline. Shifting mindsets from a punitive approach to one of growth takes time, and this is another area where leaders can assist, engaging teachers in dialogue about the potential causes of student behavior. Hierck (2019) suggests educators employ the ABC analysis, as shown in figure 5.2. In this model,

Date	Time	Antecedent	Behavior	Consequence	Possible Function (Why is this behavior occurring?)

Source: Hierck, 2019, p. 54.

Figure 5.2: The ABC direct observation tool.

*Visit **go.SolutionTree.com/leadership** for a free reproducible version of this figure.*

teachers move away from just noticing the behavior (B) and issuing consequences (C). The strength of the model lies in teachers determining the antecedents (A) that may contribute to the behavior. Is it related to the time of day, day of the week, content, or teaching strategy? Did the teacher notice that the student arrived in an agitated state?

School administrators and leaders working with teachers to probe these questions set the tone for efforts to resolve conflict and set up a positive learning environment. To be clear, we are not suggesting an absence of consequences or a laissez-faire approach to classroom management. Instead, we emphasize that determining the root cause is a necessary step to understanding the impact of trauma in the lives of students. Consequence must be paired with instruction and empathy for growth to occur.

Provide Predictable and Consistent Learning Environments

As mentioned earlier in the book, a predictable, safe environment is essential in supporting trauma-impacted students. From the moment they arrive in the classroom, students should know their teacher's expectations. This becomes even more pronounced for students already dealing with challenges brought on by traumatic experiences. Mollie Tobin (2016) believes in the importance of repetitive, predictable strategies as being key to supporting students with self-regulation difficulties. She suggests, "It is important for educators working with traumatised children to understand the key developmental pathways that may be affected by childhood trauma" (Tobin, 2016, p. 1). Hierck (2017) explains that teachers who immediately establish daily tasks and routines show students what to expect for the day:

> Does the teacher start class with a problem of the day that students can begin to address the moment they enter or will students receive it three minutes into the start of class? Or is the start of class a little unstructured with last-minute preparation, attendance checks, retrieving copies left in the office, and general chaos that changes from day to day (or even period to period)? (p. 27)

If how class begins each day is seemingly unimportant, is it surprising that many teachers deal with students who are off task or disruptive from the outset? The lack of routine to start the class means students are expected to self-manage and initiate some form of inquiry about the day's lesson. We are certain those of you reading this last sentence already know the outcome of that expectation.

While you may start this at any time, there are clear advantages to beginning the school year by establishing routines and expectations. As Hierck (2017) notes, when attempting to establish these routines after the school year had begun, "it took more time than it would have had I begun the year off right. . . . I was reminded of the importance of beginning the school year with routines that complement my classroom values and expectations" (p. 28).

Leaders can also model the need to be consistent and predictable by ensuring they conduct their team meetings in a similar fashion. The outcomes of this approach include a calm and safe school climate, minimal stress for adults, enhanced educators' sense of belonging, and a strong foundation that helps adults with self-regulation while developing positive relationships with each other and the parent community. This does not mean that you can control all circumstances; occasionally, something might throw off your routines. In those instances, leaders must do all that they can to provide support, like we did during the COVID-19 pandemic, adjusting parameters to accommodate remote or hybrid learning.

Disrupted Attachment Styles

The second area of concern suggested by Brunzell and colleagues (2015) when working with trauma-impacted students is disrupted attachment styles. When thinking of disrupted attachment, it is helpful to consider the typical pattern of attachment students experience. A child's attachment to his or her parents or caregivers shapes how that child interacts with the world, affecting how he or she learns and forms relationships. Numerous circumstances have the potential to *disrupt* that typical pattern. It could be the loss of a parent, illness, substance abuse, domestic violence, or other circumstances that constitute ACEs. If the attachment is disrupted, the child may not develop the secure base needed to form and support relationships throughout his or her life. Educators need to address this disruption.

Two key strategies to address this issue are (1) build positive teacher-student relationships, and (2) exhibit unconditional positive regard for all students.

Build Positive Teacher-Student Relationships

If we could choose one word to describe our more than combined seventy years as educators, the word would be *relationships*. Educators who build strong, positive relationships with students demonstrate that the school is populated by adults who can be trusted, genuinely care, and have students' best interests at the forefront of their actions and decisions. As leaders, think about this in terms of the team you lead. Would the same be true of your approach? Teachers focused on building positive relationships believe every student has strengths and focus less on punitive behavior management. Tom's mantra continues to be "Every student is a success story waiting to be told." Do your teachers work with their students (and do you work with your teachers) to uncover their positive attributes?

Greg Wolcott (2019) talks about the importance of recognizing that every student comes to us with his or her own unique STORY (**S**trengths, **T**endencies, **O**pportunities, **R**esources, and **Y**earnings). He goes on to say, "Capitalizing on student strengths within the classroom then, is about taking the focus off what students cannot do, and instead places the focus on what they can do" (Wolcott, 2019, p. 40). This requires teachers to recognize and focus on the things students do well and use these strengths to help them overcome challenges where more persistence is required. The same is true for each member of your team—each of them also has a STORY. It's important that you take a strengths-based approach, recognize each educator's strengths, and encourage and reinforce those strengths.

Exhibit Unconditional Positive Regard for All Students

The last thing students struggling with trauma need when they arrive at school is to encounter another adult telling them what is wrong with them. It's easily predictable as to the outcome of that scenario. Instead, students need an adult who treats them with kindness and who can empathize with the challenges they face. Being positive doesn't guarantee a result, but being negative certainly does—and it's not a result you want or need. Assuming positive intention is a skill that is underdeveloped in most of us. It's much easier to find the flaws than it is to see the beauty. Have you ever noticed how traffic slows when there is a minor fender bender? Everyone cranes their necks to get a better view of the accident. Have you ever noticed no one slows down to marvel at how well the traffic is flowing?

This notion of positive regard can also be traced back to psychologist Carl Rogers (1961). His approach exemplified what is needed when working with trauma-impacted students—a warm, caring regard for a child that is not driven by a need for satisfaction by the person providing the care. For example, if you happily say "good morning" to students every day, keep doing it because it reveals a part of you that students know and speaks to your core. If you're not that person, don't force it, because students will recognize the fakeness of the approach. After a short period of time, you'll also tire of it because you're not getting the response you want, and you'll move on to another "trick." As you lead your school toward becoming trauma sensitive, a key attribute will be this concept of unconditional positive regard for students.

Midcourse Adjustments

Imagine for a moment that the journey has begun. You and your team have done your analysis; identified opportunities for growth; clarified your current strengths; identified what tools, training, and resources you need; and taken that tentative next step. What could possibly go wrong? The answer, of course, is *plenty*! The very nature of schools, the human endeavor driven by all the interconnections that occur, means you must be open to the need for midcourse adjustments. Think about how many students arrive at your school each day. Multiply that by the number of adults working at your school. This answer gives you the total possible number of interactions each day. Now add in some of the other experiences (traumatic and otherwise) any of those individuals have gone through, and the potential for the best-laid plans going awry becomes easy to anticipate.

As you are reading this book, schools and the world at large will have experienced two significant events that severely impacted every aspect of daily life. More significantly, the events had a traumatic impact on many students and adults. First, the 2020 COVID-19 worldwide health pandemic resulted in schools closing and education occurring remotely. This meant that students who experienced trauma or were living in trauma-inducing environments were unable to access the supportive environments that schools often provide. Additionally, the impact of racial unrest resulting from the killing of people of color by law enforcement also added to the trauma experienced by students, teachers, and colleagues. We couldn't have anticipated either of these events in terms of the enormity of their impact.

By the writing of this book, the COVID-19 pandemic will have straddled three school years (beginning with the 2019–2020 school year and continuing through the 2021–2022 school year, and potentially beyond), while the conversations around racial inequity have been significantly longer. In addition to the immediate shift of focus to address those challenges, the far-reaching impact of these events not only imposed trauma on individuals in the moment, but also, for some, renewed past traumas that individuals may have thought they managed.

A second factor that may result in the need for a midcourse adjustment is what is referred to as *secondary traumatic stress* (STS). This occurs when educators are dealing with the effects of others' trauma. Their supportive role in the effort can be draining and have lasting negative effects. It is not uncommon for educators who deal with trauma-impacted students to develop their own symptoms of STS. The nature of the work can cause educators to be more susceptible to STS, especially when other factors come into play, such as personal exposure to traumatic events or to individuals who are coping with their own reactions to trauma.

Coming into direct contact with students' traumatic stories is bound to cause a reaction in educators. Educators sometimes invest so much in helping the student that they neglect themselves. This is often the nature of the work as a front-line person in the life of that student. Leaders need to be aware of the challenges and be vigilant in supporting their team while being on the watch for signs of STS.

According to the Treatment and Services Adaptation Center (n.d.), symptoms of STS might include:

- **Emotional**—feeling numb or detached; feeling overwhelmed or maybe even hopeless
- **Physical**—having low energy or feeling fatigued
- **Behavioral**—changing your routine or engaging in self-destructive coping mechanisms
- **Professional**—experiencing low performance of job tasks and responsibilities; feeling low job morale
- **Cognitive**—experiencing confusion, diminished concentration, and difficulty with decision making; experiencing trauma imagery, which is seeing events over and over again
- **Spiritual**—questioning the meaning of life or lacking self-satisfaction
- **Interpersonal**—physically withdrawing or becoming emotionally unavailable to your co-workers or your family

As you try to maintain the course you are on (following your *why*), there may develop a need for some midcourse adjustments. This should not, however, be confused with an "abandon-the-plan" approach. Responding to some of the authentic challenges previously identified might require a subtle shift in the plan, perhaps slowing down the timeline.

Plan for a Course of Action

As you look toward leading a trauma-sensitive school, it's important for you to plan out a course of action for you and your team on this journey. Stafford and Duchak (2020) identify some guidelines in figure 5.3 (page 104) as early considerations when you start planning for implementation. As mentioned previously, while all the following information may be a part of your long-term plan, it will be critical for leaders to analyze current strengths and opportunities for growth. Through that analysis, you can actualize the next steps in your journey.

Conclusion

In this chapter, we provided a variety of tools for leaders to analyze their current status and determine their first steps on the journey to becoming a trauma-sensitive school and a place of healing. You have ideas and strategies you may want to include as you develop your plan for becoming a trauma-sensitive school.

In chapter 6, we build on the information in this chapter and move beyond setting the foundation to creating a plan for implementation of trauma-sensitive practices. In addition, we focus on strategies for developing and maintaining a productive school culture that enables all students to be successful.

QUESTIONS FOR *Reflection*

As you think about what you learned in this chapter and how it can be implemented in your school, reflect on the following questions.

○ How could your school be different if it were trauma sensitive? What strategies and activities would teachers be doing that they are currently not doing?

○ To become a trauma-sensitive school, what strategies and attitudes would you need to eliminate, adopt, and enhance? How would you work with your staff to accomplish those changes?

○ What ideas and strategies did you learn in this chapter that will help you build the foundation to become a trauma-sensitive school?

A Trauma-Sensitive School *Does* . . .	A Trauma-Sensitive School *Does Not* . . .
Require all staff to be trained to understand trauma, symptoms, and its impact.	Require or encourage staff to dig deeply into the causes or sources of stress and trauma.
Recognize the importance of staff's ability to develop their own social and emotional competencies. A trauma-sensitive school will encourage and support staff as they become aware of their own biases that may interfere with developing healthy, supportive relationships with students. Staff must consistently practice and model self-regulation.	Assume that adult behavior and mindset have little or no impact on student development and behavior.
Emphasize the development of students' resiliency through: • Supportive adult relationships • Self-efficacy and perceived control • Adaptive skills and the ability to self-regulate • Sense of self-value and feeling they have something to offer others	Equate student achievement and success with proficiency in every characteristic of resiliency or social-emotional competency. Students will have these in varying degrees and that's okay (fixed versus growth mindsets).
Understand that every behavior has an underlying meaning.	Require a problem to exist before students have access to trauma-sensitive services.
Prioritize the development of social and emotional competencies that foster resilience.	Insist or imply a student with signs of stress or trauma will "get over it." Honor and validate the student's experience.
Promote and foster schoolwide connectedness and the development of supportive adult relationships.	Encourage a "just don't do it" approach to discipline. In other words, don't be reactionary and power driven. Ask, "What happened?" before rushing to consequences.
Create safety through routines, structure, predictability, and equity.	Forgo opportunities for consistency even when faced with conflict, change, or stress.
Utilize restorative disciplinary practices that keep a student in school and work to rebuild damaged relationships and understand the motivation of the behavior.	Punish most behaviors by excluding a student from class, school, or extracurricular activities.

Source: Adapted from Stafford & Duchak, 2020. Used with permission.

Figure 5.3: School-based, trauma-sensitive care.

chapter six

Planning the Trauma-Sensitive Journey for Your School

At Northbound High School, the staff have been experiencing increasing issues and challenges with the students. Over the last five years, more and more students are having difficulty staying on task for extended periods of time. Teachers report that more students are turning in either late homework or no homework at all. The staff also have noticed that more students at Northbound seem stressed. It also is evident that staff are increasingly more stressed and reacting to issues rather than trying to problem solve with students. Teachers' reactionary responses are causing the office referral rate to dramatically increase.

Principal Anne Suss knows that something has to be done to help the staff understand what might be causing these changes and how they could work to help students be successful. She adds a topic related to these issues to the building instructional leadership team's upcoming meeting agenda. This group is comprised of leaders from all the school curriculum areas, special education teachers, school counselors, as well as Principal Suss and an assistant principal who is responsible for student discipline.

At the leadership team meeting, there is a detailed discussion of student and teacher issues. One of the school counselors shares that he has seen an increase in students experiencing stress. Many of these students have shared home-related situations that impact their ability to concentrate in class and get their work done. Another school counselor reports that at a recent countywide counselor meeting, colleagues reported an increase in family-related issues, such as poverty, neglect, abuse, and other factors. She relates that other schools are experiencing issues similar to Northbound High School.

The building instructional leadership team recommends that Principal Suss look into some options for the staff to consider to begin to address these issues in the school.

In this scenario, Principal Suss takes the information and data she has about the issues at the school and involves the building instructional leadership team. In the past, this team has been helpful in addressing issues and is seen as credible by the rest of the staff. Also, by involving the leadership team in examining and then coming up with ideas to address the issues, she is developing buy-in for their proposed ideas. In the past, Principal Suss has noticed that the staff's perceptions of ideas generated by the building instructional leadership team (their peers and colleagues) were generally more favorable than of ideas she suggested. Taking advantage of buy-in would help Principal Suss to more successfully launch and sustain a change or improvement effort. She is also taking advantage of the collaborative culture that has been in place at Northbound High School to make sure the staff support each other in any changes suggested.

The most successful projects start off on the right foot. In this chapter, you'll learn ideas and strategies to begin the implementation of trauma-sensitive practices and how to move your school forward to becoming a trauma-sensitive school. As you read the information in this chapter, be sure to focus on:

- Similarities between the process of transforming your school to become trauma sensitive and the school turnaround process

- Strategies and ideas to support teachers as they make changes

- Ways to motivate or work productively with staff who pose difficulties or want to stop the school transformation

- The role of celebration, re-evaluation, and adjustments in helping make the school successful in its journey to become trauma sensitive

- Other strategies and ideas to help you move forward on your journey to becoming trauma sensitive

Since moving toward becoming a trauma-sensitive school requires new ways of thinking and behaving on the part of teachers and staff, the journey can be similar to moving a school to improved academics. We'll use some of the same terms and processes you may be familiar with in the next section featuring a model for school turnaround.

A Model for Change

In *Flip This School*, Eller and Eller (2019) present an outline for guidance in turning around a failing school. Since moving from a traditional school to one that is trauma sensitive may require a similar transformation, figure 6.1 offers four steps or recommendations that can help guide the process. The original Eller and Eller (2019) school turnaround process has been adjusted to reflect a focus on change related to becoming a trauma-sensitive school.

---

1. Signal the need for dramatic change with strong leadership.
2. Maintain a consistent focus on implementing the key practices needed to become a trauma-sensitive school.
3. Select visible improvements early in the process that are easiest to secure.
4. Build a staff committed to doing the work needed to continue the journey to becoming a trauma-sensitive school.

Source: Adapted from Eller & Eller, 2019.

Figure 6.1: Steps for guiding the process to becoming a trauma-sensitive school.

Originally, these four steps were helpful in turning around schools facing academic challenges. Let's see how they apply to the transformation from traditional to trauma sensitive.

Signal the Need for Dramatic Change With Strong Leadership

This step is similar to the initial step in turning around a school. The leadership of the school needs to inform the staff that the school is experiencing issues related to student success; be clear about the need to eliminate practices that are unproductive, and explain that you will be implementing new, trauma-sensitive practices. Usually, the need for change is based on data that have been gathered and analyzed showing student success issues. You can gather and analyze data related to students' social-emotional needs, such as office referral rates, student discipline issues, work completion rates, school counselor intervention trends, and other trauma-related data.

School staff can use the same process for gathering and analyzing trauma-related data that they use to gather and analyze academic achievement data. In the scenario that follows, let's see how Principal Jones communicates the need for change at Monroe Middle School.

> As a part of his initial work at Monroe Middle School, Principal Jones examines the data related to office referrals, suspensions, and student absences. He notices that a high number of students are missing class because of outbursts and disruptions. Almost one-third of the students has three or more office referrals each semester.

> When he shares the data with his building leadership team, team members are surprised by the information. Many students they identify as most needy are missing significant amounts of class time. Also, some patterns emerge related to the office referrals and suspensions. Many of these are related to issues of disrespect, emotional outbursts, and other aspects of trauma.

> Now that Principal Jones established a foundation of common information, he helps the leadership team understand the impact of trauma and the idea of a trauma-sensitive school. This process takes some time, but he knows it will be important to develop what John Kotter (2012) calls a guiding coalition to help support the changes needed at Monroe. A guiding coalition is the group of teachers who will be committed to the change and help to guide their colleagues through the change.

> Once Principal Jones builds the understanding and leadership capacity of the leadership team, he works with team members to conduct staff meetings to share the data and strategies to move the school toward becoming trauma sensitive. Principal Jones takes the lead in presenting the data and the need for change but uses his leadership team for support. After presenting the referral and suspension data, he asks each team member to facilitate small-group conversations. In these small groups, teachers can ask questions, share concerns, and discuss what they need to do to move toward consensus and change the operations at Monroe.

> At the end of the meeting, Principal Jones sums up the need for the change and lets the staff know that he will work with the leadership team to develop an implementation plan.

In this example, Principal Jones demonstrates one way to announce the need for change. He decides to involve his building leadership team from the start as a way to develop buy-in for the idea. Having small groups review the data helps everyone see the need for change.

In some other schools, the leader may just share the trauma-related data and the plan for change with the staff. However the need for change is communicated, it needs to be clear that the old way of doing business cannot continue.

In communicating the need for change, be sure to include the following:

- Clear identification of the issue or problem (normally based on data analysis)
- A clear plan you will use to implement the needed changes in moving forward with trauma-sensitive planning and strategies

Announcing the need for change also provides the rationale and motivation for the change. Kotter (2012) calls this *establishing a sense of urgency*. The data presented by Principal Jones were intended to develop a sense of urgency for the leadership team to move the trauma-sensitive focus forward. A sense of urgency is foundational for successful change. Without a sense of urgency, few changes are successful.

Maintain a Consistent Focus on Implementing the Key Practices Needed to Become a Trauma-Sensitive School

The second step in becoming a trauma-sensitive school is to focus on the techniques and strategies that will address the needs of trauma-impacted students. This step takes place during the planning of the trauma-sensitive change project and needs to continue through the initial implementation and eventually become part of the school culture. Following this step means that the trauma-sensitive change will not just consist of social-emotional lessons conducted once a week for a semester. Instead, trauma-sensitive strategies and practices must be integrated within the curriculum so they become the "way we do business" rather than isolated incidents.

To effectively integrate trauma-sensitive practices, it's important to pair them with academic content. For example, let's say that one of the needs your school leadership team identifies is to improve the consistency in classroom routines. One of the agreed-on routines is for all teachers to greet students at the door at the beginning of class and have an activity for students to start when they enter the classroom. This activity should have an academic focus, such as a few review questions about the previous day's academic content. When the teacher starts the class, he or she can review and comment on the behavior students are demonstrating (getting to work right away) in addition to the academic content (the review). This helps students see how the behavior (getting to work right away) is tied to the academic skills they are practicing.

In another example, suppose that teachers in an elementary setting all decide to focus on holding morning meetings with their classes to set the tone, assess student mood, and build community. During these morning meetings, it's important for teachers to have students engage in academic learning (for example, counting, talking about how to give peer feedback in writing, and so on). By talking about academics while practicing the procedures of sitting and discussing, teachers tie the academics to a consistent routine. The students start to learn both the learning process (the behavior skill) and the academic content.

Maintaining a consistent focus on improving instruction involves the integration or marriage between the content and the learning processes. Trauma-sensitive schools may decide to focus on a small number of common strategies everyone can implement. This is the concept we'll discuss in step 3, select visible improvements early in the process that are easiest to secure.

In the scenario, the staff at Monroe Middle School work on the foundational processes to build relationships with students. They also develop strategies to assess students' emotional states in each classroom. Once they implement these foundational techniques, the school chooses a few others to implement.

Select Visible Improvements Early in the Process That Are Easiest to Secure

Step 3 of the change process builds on step 2. In step 3, the leaders and the faculty of the school select a small number of trauma-sensitive strategies to implement that they think will be the most visible and easiest to implement successfully. For example, let's say the building leadership team has determined that the implementation of trauma-sensitive practices should start by focusing on one building's relationships between faculty and students. Initially, they could decide to have teachers do three things: (1) send a welcome postcard to their students, (2) greet every student when he or she comes into the classroom, and (3) provide a place for students to meet (like open gym) in the morning. At this meeting place, faculty members could stop in and informally talk with students in order to build relationships. They could easily learn and track their progress on these strategies.

During faculty meetings, teachers could dedicate some time to discussing the initial implementation of these three strategies. The principal could provide faculty with feedback on their implementation during walk-through observations, and teachers could share success stories on the implementation at collaborative team sessions.

Since the staff would be focusing on a small number of strategies, they can be more successful. The plans for these three strategies could be part of the goal-planning process. The narrow focus and specificity would help implementation be more successful.

Let's see how Principal Jones uses this idea as he begins to move Monroe Middle School toward becoming more trauma sensitive.

> Once the building leadership team at Monroe Middle School works with the staff to let them know about the issue of trauma and the need for change, the members work together to develop an initial implementation plan. For this initial plan, the team focuses on two areas: building positive relationships and reducing teacher-student conflict escalation. The team believes these two areas would be highly visible and could build on the existing skill level of the faculty.
>
> The team develops a process in which students could come to school before the start of the formal school day to relax, play in the gym, read, and so on. The staff divide up the supervision of these activities so there is time for teachers to visit with and get to know students and build relationships.
>
> In the second area, reducing conflict, the team finds a video training program related to conflict de-escalation. It offers opportunities for teachers to participate in the program based on their schedules and offers professional development credits for their participation. Principal Jones and his assistants visit classrooms and reinforce the content with teachers. Instructional coaches are able to provide support as well.
>
> While there are still some issues, overall, conflicts are reduced. Principal Jones and the leadership team share the data related to conflicts and work with teachers to make midcourse adjustments based on the data and teacher feedback. As the environment improves, the school holds small celebrations to recognize the

staff's hard work. Once the school implements these two founda-
tional strategies, they are able to introduce new strategies.

In this example, the Monroe Middle School staff start their trauma-sensitive journey using a small number of strategies and then build on them to add more complex strategies later. This process allows the staff to gradually move toward becoming trauma sensitive.

Build a Staff Committed to Doing the Work Needed to Continue the Journey to Becoming a Trauma-Sensitive School

Until the staff are committed to becoming trauma sensitive, the change will not be successful. In our profession, we have the concept of *buy-in*. Buy-in refers to the level of commitment staff members have in the success of the change or intervention. Without buy-in, the staff will not be willing to do the hard work needed in order to make the trauma-sensitive journey successful.

Teacher buy-in may not come naturally. Sometimes, teachers will want to continue to do the same things they've always done. The desire to avoid making changes is natural and can cause resistance on the part of your teachers. There are several strategies you can implement that increase buy-in and reduce resistance. For example, involving a building instructional leadership team (or other leadership team at the school) gives the rest of the staff a sense of buy-in since their peers are involved in creating the plan. Another example is asking teachers to share positive examples of their implementation strategies at staff meetings. In our experiences, when teachers share positive experiences about what they are doing, it makes them more committed to the success of the implementation.

In the schools we lead, we notice that if we don't take time to build commitment and buy-in, some teachers spend time and energy trying to undermine and resist the new ideas. We are reminded of this quote by John Kenneth Galbraith (BrainyQuote, n.d.a): "Faced with the choice between changing one's mind and proving that there is no need to do so, almost everyone gets busy on the proof."

One way to make sure your staff are committed to the change is to develop a shared vision. We presented this strategy earlier, but it's so important it bears repeating. When people are involved in understanding the issues and assisting in designing the solutions, they tend to be more committed to the success of the change. James Kouzes and Barry Posner (2017) identify the importance of developing shared vision as a way of developing ownership. When you own something, you take better care of it and want to be successful. In the example of Principal Jones, he used the concept of shared vision when he involved the building leadership team to develop the initial change plan for a trauma-sensitive school. He also used this idea when he asked team members to facilitate small groups of faculty in understanding the school data and providing the opportunity for them to ask questions and share concerns. By involving teachers in the data analysis and holding conversations about the possible plans to address the issues, he engaged them with the plan rather than dictating it to them. Engagement is one key component to developing a shared vision.

Other Strategies to Consider for a Successful Trauma-Sensitive Journey

The four steps previously described will provide a good foundation to build your trauma-sensitive school change effort. However, those four steps will not be enough to sustain your trauma-sensitive effort. Following are some other factors that can help your school be more successful in becoming trauma sensitive.

School Culture and Attitude, or the Care Factor

From our own experiences and from the teachers we have supported in becoming trauma-sensitive instructors, relationships are an important part of reaching out to students impacted by trauma. Theodore Roosevelt summed up this concept with this famous quote: "People don't care how much you know until they know how much you care" (Goodreads, n.d.). It's clear that knowledge is important, but how much we care is even more important. In *Flip This School*, Eller and Eller (2019) describe the importance of the *care factor*. The care factor is how you show people that you care about them. The care factor helps people feel they are valued and a valuable part of the organization. Feeling valued and a part of the organization motivates people to want to help the organization be successful. Using the care factor also contributes to the short-term climate and long-term culture of the school. Both of these elements help to increase the success of the school change effort and the journey toward becoming trauma sensitive. We have found that when people feel valued and important, they are more committed to the success of the school.

The Care Factor for Staff

In his work with teachers getting their master's in teacher leadership, John has had teachers complete an activity in which they identify significant experiences and memories from their prekindergarten through high school years. More than 99 percent of the responses included items such as the following.

- Teachers taking an interest in them

- Teachers reaching out and encouraging them

- Teachers helping them address a problem

- Teachers helping them make more of themselves than they thought they were capable of becoming

- Other supportive and related experiences

All of these and the other memories and experiences identified by these teachers are related to the *care factor*.

Since several of the original ACEs factors (such as neglect and abuse) are related to a lack of caring on the part of adults in students' lives, students may not experience the caring that some others do. In our personal situations, our parents were absorbed by their own issues and not able to show they cared. If you can show that you care (in an appropriate manner), some trauma-impacted students can get the message that significant adults in their world do care about them.

In our experiences, it's important that we as leaders show our faculty that we care about them. If our staff feel that we care, it may be easier for them to show students they care. Strategies to develop the care factor with your staff could include the following.

- Sincerely telling them you care about them and their success

- Being willing to talk with them about topics not related to school (for example, hobbies, sports, topics related to their interests, and so on)

- Being transparent when making decisions

- Getting to know staff beyond what they do at work

- Recognizing birthdays, anniversaries, and other special events

- Getting to know their families and taking an interest in them

- Covering their duties and classes to give them a break

- Providing a forum for listening to their aspirations and concerns
- Using personal regard when talking with them
- Being honest and open with them when providing feedback

In the schools we have led, we have used a modified interest inventory to find out information about the lives of staff outside the school setting. These sorts of inventories ask staff to identify important aspects related to their teaching and areas outside school, including the following.

- Important dates or events in their lives
- Important people in their lives
- Hobbies or interests they have outside of school
- Passions related to their teaching
- Other topics you may find interesting to know

Sometimes, we have talked about interests of staff members in a one-on-one person meeting held with each staff member in the summer or early fall. We have also used an interest survey that staff complete and return to the office. Consider different ways you can learn more about your staff in the manner that makes the most sense for you and is the most comfortable for them.

Building the care factor before making changes is ideal, but you can develop it at any point in the trauma-sensitive school journey.

The Care Factor for Students

In addition to helping faculty develop buy-in and commitment, the care factor is an essential practice in working with students. Because of the nature of most ACE issues, many trauma-impacted students do not have a caring adult in their lives. If teachers work in an environment where they feel cared for, it will be easier for them to develop a similar sense of caring for their students.

Bruce Perry (n.d.), a pioneering neuroscientist in the field of trauma, offers the following three steps to connecting with vulnerable, trauma-impacted students. He calls these the three Rs to reaching the learning brain: (1) regulate, (2) relate, and (3) reason.

> First: We must help the child to regulate and calm their fight/flight/
> freeze responses.

Second: We must relate and connect with the child through an attuned and sensitive relationship.

Third: We can support the child to reflect, learn, remember, articulate and become self-assured. (Perry, n.d.)

Perry (n.d.) notes that "heading straight for the 'reasoning' part of the brain with an expectation of learning will not work so well if the child is dysregulated and disconnected from others."

By actively integrating trauma-sensitive care into its culture and practices, a school can move from being trauma reactive (whereby they might be inducing more trauma) to creating a healing environment for students and staff that might reduce trauma. This is all part of the care factor for students.

Additionally, encourage teachers to find out more about their students through the use of interest inventories or meeting individually to get to know them. Teachers can do the following to get to know their students.

- Reach out to students before the start of the school year. The initial contact could be through the phone, email, or sending a postcard.

- Use the first two weeks of school to build relationships with students. In addition to teaching initial routines and procedures, teachers can set up individual or small-group meeting times to talk to and get to know more about their students.

- Have students complete an interest inventory so you can learn more about them and discover some of their interests. Some teachers use a paper-and-pencil form, while others use technology-supported forms that allow students to complete surveys online. Completing interest inventories can be integrated with teaching routines and procedures to allow students to practice these routines in an academic-related task.

Teachers might ask students to provide information that could be interesting for students to share with the class, such as the following.

  ○ Significant dates (birthday, special days)

  ○ Hobbies and other personal interests

  ○ Favorite books, movies, video games, and so on

  ○ How they like to learn

○ Appropriate personal information, such as family members, close friends, family pets, and so on

Observe students as they interact with each other during classroom activities and informal conversations in class. You can see a lot if you watch and make note of what you're seeing. As you move forward in your journey to becoming a trauma-sensitive school, showing staff and students you care needs to become a central part of your plan.

Celebrations

An essential aspect of your trauma-sensitive journey must include celebrating your success. Just like a mountain climber who needs to periodically stop and celebrate his or her progress while scaling almost impossible peaks, you need to periodically stop, take stock in your accomplishments, and enjoy your successes.

Teachers often can feel overworked and underappreciated. This became even more evident as schools dealt with the impacts of the COVID-19 pandemic. Many were working long hours outside of school, using some of their own money to purchase supplies and materials, and spending a lot of their emotional resources working with the students at school. Asking them to take on even more without some type of reward can seem daunting.

An essential part of any successful change effort and one way to develop buy-in is to build celebrations into your trauma-sensitive school journey. Celebrations serve as a type of reward for the hard work people put into making a change.

In *Creative Strategies to Transform School Culture*, Eller and Eller (2009) discuss the role and importance of celebrations in shaping the school culture. Celebrations build a school culture where people feel valued and appreciated. They also serve to reduce barriers and help staff enjoy their work and each other.

Since educators are not accustomed to celebrating, it's a good idea to build in periodic celebrations during the planning process when working to make your school more trauma sensitive. Similar to the earlier attribute of planning for small, easily-attainable victories, you'll want to have fairly regular celebrations. Following is a sample schedule for one school that recently focused on becoming more trauma sensitive.

- August: Trauma-sensitive staff kickoff celebration
- Mid-September: One-month implementation celebration

- Early November: First-quarter celebration

- Late January: Semester celebration

- Early March: Spring celebration

- May or June: End-of-year-one celebration

In this example, the faculty held six celebrations. Most of these celebrations were fairly simple, and several were actually organized by the building instructional leadership team. For example, the August kickoff celebration was a part of a regularly scheduled faculty meeting. At the celebration, the meeting room was decorated, there was cake and coffee available, and members of the building leadership team spoke about their excitement related to the trauma-sensitive project. The cake and decorations were paid for by the school parent-teacher organization. The kickoff celebration set a tone of excitement in the school. Many of the teachers said they had never had a kickoff celebration in the past. Holding a celebration like this also illustrated the importance of the upcoming trauma-sensitive project. In addition to setting a positive and appreciative tone, celebrations serve to show the importance of a project or initiative.

Schools that may not have large budgets to reward teachers can still hold small and meaningful celebrations to build commitment and motivate teachers to keep working and stay the course. Strategies such as providing treats at a staff meeting and complementing teachers for their progress, holding all-school assemblies to announce major accomplishments, providing small prizes based on random drawings, covering teacher duties, and other small celebrations can go a long way in letting teachers know you appreciate their hard work and commitment.

Strategies to Move Beyond the Initial Focus on Trauma-Sensitive Instruction

In addition to the four steps presented in figure 6.1 (page 107) and the strategies shared in the previous section, there are several other considerations you'll want to include in your trauma-sensitive journey. These are not necessarily steps in the implementation process but things you should consider when moving forward on your trauma-sensitive journey.

- **Provide opportunities for continual learning and discussion of the concept of trauma-sensitive schools and practices:**
  Frequent conversations and information related to the concept of

trauma-sensitive instruction are needed to move the implementation plan forward. This high level of engagement allows teachers to understand and refine their understanding of trauma-sensitive instruction. This continual learning could be in the form of professional development, conversations and presentations at staff meetings, teachers sharing successful lessons and experiences they've had related to trauma-sensitive instruction, short professional development mini-sessions held before or after school, collaborative teams discussing successful strategies at their periodic meetings, class coverage during the day allowing staff to learn more ideas, and other job-embedded professional development strategies.

- **Provide opportunities for staff to meet and talk about the problem areas that are emerging during their trauma-sensitive journey:** Just like it's important to schedule periodic celebrations, it's also important to schedule regular times to meet to talk about issues that arise or aspects of the implementation that are not going well. Two important items need to be included in these types of meetings: (1) the opportunity to identify the problems or issues, and (2) the opportunity to generate solutions for these issues. If both of these items are not planned for, follow-up sessions can turn into "gripe sessions" where nothing is accomplished except for venting.

To help keep these types of meetings focused on problem solving, we structure them to ensure they produce solutions. Following is a sample problem-solving meeting agenda.

1. At the beginning of the meeting, state the purpose for the meeting (to identify and generate solutions to problems).

2. Break the large group into small conversational groups of four to five people.

3. Give each small group a T-chart that has a vertical line down the middle. Title the left column *Problems* and the right column *Solutions*. Give the groups a few minutes to generate and write down two to three problems and solutions to these problems. Ask each group to share its list with the whole group. You can make a master list or chart showing the points presented by each small group.

4. At the end of the activity, the whole group can select two to three
    areas from the master chart they want to address in the next month.
    The group can also engage in discussions about resources or assets they
    can use to address the issues.

By carefully structuring the meeting, you can help the staff to engage in problem solving while keeping the focus on implementing trauma-sensitive strategies
and practices.

- **Know your leadership strengths and limitations:** Take time to
  identify and understand your leadership strengths and limitations.
  You will find it helpful to understand leadership power bases and how
  to use them. You'll want to understand how you respond to conflict
  and chaos. When things seem to be falling apart around you, how
  do you react? Do you have the sense of calmness needed to endure
  challenging situations but the impatience to not become satisfied with
  the status quo?

- **Diagnose the challenge you are about to take on and how the
  school can be changed:** Examine the strengths and challenges at
  the school to determine how you can move forward on the trauma-
  sensitive journey. What are the strengths and capacities available
  within the school community? Do you have the resources (both
  monetary and human) that you'll need to support the changes? Can
  the hard decisions you'll need to make be supported? These and
  many other considerations should be contemplated as you move your
  implementation plan forward.

- **Plan for, provide, or find the resources you'll need to support
  the trauma-sensitive journey:** Without the necessary resources, the
  trauma-sensitive journey will be difficult if not impossible. In your
  planning, you'll need to consider both monetary and human resources.
  For example, to implement new trauma-sensitive teaching strategies,
  teachers will need professional development and coaching. By setting
  aside the funding to support these strategies, you're ensuring that
  implementation will be more successful.

- **Build leadership capacity at the teacher level:** You'll quickly find that you can't transform the school all by yourself. You'll need to develop leadership structures at the school that engage others in understanding the issues, developing plans, communicating these plans to their colleagues, and supporting them as they implement these plans. Your leadership efforts may start with the development of a *building instructional leadership team* and eventually expanding the leadership to include the entire staff. By building leadership capacity, others feel like they are a part of the process. Once you build this leadership, the changes can be self-sustaining and long term.

- **Continue to refine the working climate of the school to develop a positive school culture:** As the trauma-sensitive transformation process unfolds, people can become tired and discouraged. It will be important for you to work with a leadership group (like the building leadership team) to implement strategies that positively impact the working climate at the school. Even though people are working hard, they can have fun and feel a sense of satisfaction. Over time, this working climate will impact the school culture. Once a culture of success has started to develop, the school will continue to develop in a positive direction.

- **Identify and deal with trouble areas of the implementation as they start to deteriorate:** As trauma-sensitive implementation continues, you'll soon find that issues will arise, things will not go as planned, and unanticipated things will happen. This is why it's important to carefully monitor the implementation and troubleshoot issues that you and your leadership team encounter.

- **Keep moving forward to identify and tackle new challenges:** Once you attain initial project goals, you will need to keep the staff focused while introducing new areas for growth and development. While implementing changes and seeing student success can be exciting and motivating, it can also be tiring to address the deficits at the school. Provide consistent encouragement and motivation as implementation unfolds.

Conclusion

In this chapter, we discussed some of the ideas and strategies to help move the transformation to a trauma-sensitive school from planning to implementation. Your school may go through phases or steps in this process. We used the comparison of operating a turnaround school to changing from a traditional school to one that is trauma sensitive because of the similarities in the level of change needed. Your school may need more or fewer changes, but with a basic model, you can adjust your implementation processes.

In starting your trauma-sensitive school journey, thinking and planning are important aspects to consider. Be sure that you've thought through both the assets you'll use and the issues you'll encounter in order to make the journey.

In the next chapter, we discuss issues that may arise during implementation that could derail your progress. In some cases, these are issues you might anticipate, and you can be proactive to minimize their negative impacts. In other cases, they may be issues you haven't considered.

QUESTIONS FOR *Reflection*

As you think about what you learned in this chapter and how it can be implemented in your school, reflect on the following questions.

○ Why is communicating the need for a dramatic change an important part of the change process? What are some strategies you can use to communicate the need for change to the school community?

○ Why is developing a shared vision or buy-in so important to the change process? How can a school leadership team be helpful in developing a sense of buy-in in staff members?

○ How can assessing your own strengths and resources help you implement trauma-sensitive leadership? Why would a leader want to take the time to complete a self-assessment before moving forward on a trauma-sensitive school project?

chapter seven

Launching and Sustaining Trauma-Sensitive Practices in Your School

It's May at Dakota Elementary School, and Principal Fountaine is making plans to continue working to meet the needs of trauma-impacted students. She works tirelessly with the teachers and staff members to help them to provide safe and predictable structures to help trauma-impacted and all other students be successful. Her major efforts focus on helping reshape the attitudes and beliefs of the staff. Negative attitudes about the students, their backgrounds, their families, and other factors used to prevail. She no longer wants the school to be a place where adults gather to gripe and complain. During the recent virtual learning experience, the staff have a window into their students' homes. Many of the staff comment that they now have a greater understanding of some of the situations their students face on a daily basis.

Principal Fountaine supports the staff by working with collaborative teacher teams to implement trauma-sensitive practices. Her school leadership team sets three specific goals for trauma-sensitive practices and then develops specific plans to support their teachers. During the weekly meetings, collaborative teams study and evaluate strategies by discussing their implementation efforts and design strategies to address any problems or issues they encounter. Some of the collaborative teams problem solve by talking, while others use data they gathered regarding student engagement, student evaluations (descriptions of the learning environment), and classroom observations from visiting each other's classrooms. Many teachers are able to successfully implement several strategies because of the support of their peers. It's now time to plan how to use this first year as a foundation to build on for continued success in becoming trauma sensitive.

Principal Fountaine faces a task that many principals face. Her school has had initial success in implementing trauma-sensitive practices, but how can the staff continue their implementation for the success of all students? What do they need to do to move the school to a new and higher level of implementation? How will they avoid what some leaders refer to as *implementation dip*, moving backward rather than forward? All these and other potential problems face leaders as they try to make trauma-sensitive practices a part of the long-term school culture.

In this chapter, you'll learn about ideas and strategies that you can implement to build on the first year's success of your trauma-sensitive journey.

As you review this chapter, you'll learn more about the following.

- Strategies and techniques to move the trauma-sensitive implementation beyond the planning stage for long-term success

- How the change process can cause problems during a trauma-sensitive journey

- How to successfully navigate the issues caused by the change process

- The importance of gathering data to assess the effectiveness of the implementation

- How to conduct problem-solving meetings to help keep the implementation moving forward in a productive manner

These strategies will help you lead your school beyond the newness of helping the staff implement trauma-sensitive instruction and practices and will help the school actually become a trauma-sensitive place for students and staff. In the end, your goal should be to positively impact the school culture to become trauma sensitive.

Navigation of the Change Process

In the initial efforts to move your school toward a trauma-sensitive school, you may have used a concise or even informal plan. You may have relied on a small number of dedicated, informal leaders to guide the implementation. In a way, this approach could have been similar to piloting or trying out strategies. Principals in first-year projects encourage staff to try a small number of strategies and see how they work.

In a continued or sustained implementation that builds on an initial trial, a more formal planning process is needed. In *Flip This School*, Eller and Eller (2019) provide a step-by-step process for leading a school improvement effort. Moving a school to become trauma sensitive is a type of school improvement process. One difference between a school improvement effort and a trauma-sensitive effort may be the focus of the change. In a trauma-sensitive effort, you will be helping teachers focus beyond just academics to look at their attitudes and behaviors, the procedures and processes for their classroom and the entire school, and ways of developing a safe, predictable, calm environment. Over time, these trauma-sensitive practices will positively impact academic achievement.

Since the processes used by leaders and schools to become trauma sensitive are similar to those used to address academic issues, we offer a modified version of the process from *Flip This School* (Eller & Eller, 2019), as shown in figure 7.1. Keep these elements in mind as you move beyond your initial planning and work to transform your school to become more trauma sensitive.

- Understand yourself as a leader and the strengths and limitations of your staff.
- Understand essential actions and strategies related to trauma-sensitive teaching.
- Understand how the change process will impact your trauma-sensitive efforts.
- Gather data related to your initial trauma-sensitive efforts.
- Develop both intermediate and long-term goals and objectives for your trauma-sensitive efforts.
- Develop strategies to gather data related to the trauma-sensitive implementation.
- Develop strategies to continue to develop a collaborative culture and a positive working environment.
- Develop strategies to work through problems and issues that arise during implementation.
- Build capacity within your staff.
- Successfully manage issues related to change.
- Plan celebrations for success.

Source: Adapted from Eller & Eller, 2019.

Figure 7.1: Considerations for leading a trauma-sensitive school.

Even though these elements are presented in a sequence, you can adjust the order to match your needs. Let's take a more detailed look at a few of these elements.

Understand Yourself as a Leader and the Strengths and Limitations of Your Staff

Successful implementation in relation to building a trauma-sensitive school requires that you take stock of what you bring as a leader and the strengths and limitations of your staff. If you understand your leadership strengths, you'll be able to decide how to lead the project. If you are comfortable leading out in front, you'll use that strategy. Instead, if you prefer to develop leaders within your school, you can use that approach.

Previously, we mentioned that principals find that using a building leadership team and integrating the plan into a collaborative team environment is an effective way to support change efforts. If you are good at leading from the front, you might be the leader of the building leadership team. If you prefer to develop leadership within the faculty, you might choose to have a staff member lead that team while you serve as a member. Understanding your strengths and challenges as a leader will help you determine the best ways to move forward.

Having a clear understanding of the strengths and limitations of the staff as well is crucial to the success of the implementation. This understanding will help you work with them developmentally, focusing on their strengths while building their skills in needed areas. For example, if most staff members have skills in trauma-sensitive practices, you may want to have them share their knowledge with each other. You may have some teachers conduct mini-sessions in which they share successful trauma-sensitive practices with other teachers. This strategy would build the collective skills of all teachers. If you find that most staff members lack a basic understanding (or commitment) to trauma-sensitive practices, you may want to bring in experts from outside the school to provide professional development to build those basic skills. Once you provide a foundation of trauma-sensitive information, you may be able to have teachers observe and coach each other. These are just two examples to build on the strengths of your staff during your trauma-sensitive journey.

Understand Essential Actions and Strategies Related to Trauma-Sensitive Teaching

To be successful with trauma-sensitive instruction and practices, teachers must have a thorough understanding of the rationale and theories behind them and the essential attitudes and processes. In *Trauma-Sensitive Instruction* (Eller & Hierck, 2021), you'll find many strategies you can work on with your staff. With this strong background, you'll be able to decide what needs to be addressed initially and what needs follow-up as you implement the process. For example, since the ability to change attitudes is foundational, you may want to spend time talking about this element with your building leadership team and your collaborative teacher teams. In an initial implementation, you may be able to move forward with staff understanding and implementing a small number of common strategies. In the second and subsequent years, you'll want them to have a strong base of understanding to build on.

In *Flip This School*, Eller and Eller (2019) discuss the work of Shirley M. Hord, William L. Rutherford, Leslie Huling-Austin, and Gene E. Hall (1987) and their concerns-based adoption model (CBAM). The model describes several stages of concern that can help school leaders understand the needs of staff members during a change and respond to the concerns their staff members may express. It's hard for teachers and staff members to move to the next level of change if the needs at an earlier level are not addressed. For example, if staff members don't have a basic awareness of what they are implementing, it's hard for them to understand how the change will impact them personally. By listening to staff during a change, you can gain a basic understanding of the various concern levels that need to be addressed.

Following are the basic stages of the CBAM for change (Hord et al., 1987).

1. **Awareness stage:** Having basic knowledge about the new expectations, practices, or strategies.

2. **Information stage:** Possessing specific knowledge about the new expectations, practices, or strategies. Also, understanding specific details like the implementation schedule, the reasoning and rationale behind the program components, and other more detailed aspects related to the change or implementation.

3. **Personal stage:** Having an understanding of how the change or implementation affects them and the work they do in the school.

4. **Management stage:** An understanding of how to operate or implement the strategies and techniques associated with the change or implementation.

5. **Consequences stage:** Having a clear understanding of the impact of the changes, strategies, and techniques on the students and on student learning and achievement.

6. **Collaboration stage:** Possessing a clear mastery of the techniques and strategies of the new innovation so that they can work with or collaborate with others in the use of these techniques and strategies.

7. **Refocusing stage:** Having a clear understanding and experience in working with the new ideas, strategies, and techniques. Using this experience to begin to make adjustments or changes in these strategies and techniques to make them fit into the culture or practices of the classroom and the school. In other words, personalizing the program. (Eller & Eller, 2019, p. 177)

Of particular importance is the information stage. Teachers need to know the details about the program they are implementing. This may be a good area to start in the trauma-sensitive implementation process. The building leadership team and the collaborative teams can work to help everyone understand the *what* of the implementation.

In trauma-sensitive school change projects, we have helped principals gather informal data that help them understand the various "levels of need" of their staff. Then, they can implement the best support strategies to help address the needs. For example, in one school's trauma-sensitive journey, the principal assessed that there were teachers in two need groups. One group of early adopters was ready to learn strategies to help them manage the trauma-sensitive strategies they had learned (management stage), while another group was still confused about the details, rationale, and basic assumptions related to trauma-sensitive instruction.

This principal offered two types of professional development mini-sessions. One set of mini-sessions covered the basic aspects of trauma-sensitive instruction. A second set of professional development mini-sessions contained content related to managing, assessing, and adjusting trauma-sensitive practices in more advanced implementations. Teachers could select the mini-sessions they attended. The teachers were able to get information related to their specific needs while moving forward on their implementation.

School leaders have found the stages-of-concern information valuable as they think about how to understand the concerns that may be getting in the way of their staff and teachers being successful in implementing trauma-sensitive instruction. It's helped them be better at personalizing the support for their teachers.

Understand How the Change Process Will Impact Your Trauma-Sensitive Efforts

In the previous section, we talked about the value of understanding stages of concern when dealing with change. The concerns-based adoption model is focused on individual needs and issues during the change process. However, it's also essential that school leaders focus on the entire organization.

While there are several models related to change, one we have found particularly helpful is the following simple and straightforward model created by John Kotter (2012).

Kotter's (2012) model helps guide staff through changes related to the entire school or organization and the stages needed for success.

1. **Establish a sense of urgency:** One of the foundational elements Kotter addresses is related to the reason or rationale for the change. Kotter (2012) calls this *establishing a sense of urgency*. In our experience, this stage is crucial because people benefit from understanding *why* they and their organization are being asked to change. A leader can provide the rationale or vision for the change, but it's important for those following to buy into the rationale or urgency. Leaders help teachers buy in or be a part of the rationale for the change through a variety of techniques, including the following.

   o Presenting the data to support the need for trauma-sensitive instruction to the staff

   o Having the building leadership team analyze the data and share the need for the trauma-sensitive school focus

   o Empowering informal or formal teacher leaders to share the need for the trauma-sensitive school journey

   o Other strategies to get colleagues involved in understanding the issues and recommending a change

2. **Form a guiding coalition:** In the second stage of the Kotter model, a small guiding coalition helps to begin with planning the change. Another aspect of a guiding coalition could involve a small group of teachers piloting several trauma-sensitive strategies and then reporting back to the larger group about how things are going. Guiding coalitions can test and try some ideas and work out potential issues related to implementation. In some implementations, the building instructional leadership team can serve as a guiding coalition.

3. **Create a vision:** Once a guiding coalition has an opportunity to get involved in the implementation, it's a good time for the leader, the building instructional leadership team, and potentially the entire staff to get involved in refining the vision for the trauma-sensitive journey. This new, refined vision will incorporate the original rationale plus any new insights identified during the guiding coalition's work.

4. **Communicate the vision:** Now that the vision for your trauma-sensitive journey has been refined, it's important to communicate it to all stakeholders. Communication methods should include a variety of techniques and strategies, such as creating printed plans, having face-to-face meetings, reaching out to the school community, sharing details about your trauma-sensitive journey with advisory groups, and so on. The more communication that takes place, the more stakeholders understand why you are implementing certain strategies and processes. Also, publicly stating your intentions can help increase accountability since the school leaders have told others what they plan to do.

5. **Empower others:** Once the project has been launched, building teacher capacity is the way we empower educators for success. Providing ongoing professional development and follow-up support through strategies, such as coaching, ensures everyone has the skills to be successful. Empowering others also involves helping your staff build a commitment to the success of the project.

6. **Create short-term wins:** Identifying easy wins and focusing on short-term success provides quick results and helps people stay motivated. In some of the scenarios provided in this book, we illustrated the idea of quick wins or focusing on strategies that can be implemented

rather quickly. These types of strategies give people the immediate feedback they need to stay motivated to keep working on the trauma-sensitive journey.

7. **Consolidate wins:** In consolidating wins, school leaders and building leadership team members find a way to tie together the early victories in the implementation process. Sometimes, this consolidation also includes celebrations and opportunities to affirm the early successes. By celebrating successes, school leaders help teachers see the fruits of their labor and keep focused on moving forward on the trauma-sensitive journey.

8. **Make changes part of the organizational culture:** After the initial implementation successes, it's important that trauma-sensitive strategies become a part of the school culture. The school culture enables the most important elements to become the "way the school does business." Building a culture may take several years, but it will ensure that the essential practices continue to be implemented and positively impact student success.

Gather Data Related to Your Initial Trauma-Sensitive Efforts

Just like it's crucial to gather data about student achievement related to school change or turnaround efforts, it's crucial to do the same to start the journey to becoming a trauma-sensitive school. Some data related to the change to becoming a trauma-sensitive school may be similar to data gathered for other school change efforts (academic achievement, absenteeism, office referrals, and so on). However, you may need to identify other, more unique data (time needed to get classes started, levels of student withdrawal from class, level of disruptions or outbursts, and other trauma-related elements) to fully inform your trauma-sensitive implementation.

Here are several data sources you may want to consider in using to inform your trauma-sensitive implementation.

- **Amount of time it takes to get classes started:** If classes are getting started sooner, the practices may be working.

- **Number of office referrals:** If office referrals are going down, trauma-sensitive strategies and efforts to improve teacher attitudes may be working.

- **Number of students disconnecting from classroom instruction in a period:** If teachers are reporting improved student engagement, their instructional strategies may be making a positive difference.

- **Number of student visits to the school counselor:** Depending on the frequency and reasons for the visits, your strategies may be working. For example, if the school trauma-sensitive project is focusing on counselors becoming more of a resource for students and teachers, then an increase in visits would be a good thing.

- **Number of tardies:** If class tardies are decreasing, that may indicate success with trauma-sensitive strategies.

- **Number of bus referrals:** If bus discipline referrals are decreasing, this might indicate that your trauma-sensitive strategies are working.

- **Number of student outbursts in class:** Like other disruptions shared earlier, fewer may indicate an improvement in the school climate from the implementation of trauma-sensitive practices.

The types of data you choose to gather will depend on the specific situations you are facing in your particular school. It will be fruitful for you to involve others in identifying the best types of data to gather and use as you carry out your trauma-sensitive implementation.

You'll want to use the same type of data you identified in launching your implementation in measuring its success as it unfolds. This consistency ensures that you get an accurate assessment of the progress you're making in transforming your school toward becoming trauma sensitive.

Develop Both Intermediate and Long-Term Goals and Objectives for Your Trauma-Sensitive Efforts

Clear, written, and focused goals are essential to the success of a trauma-sensitive school plan. We are sure that you've heard of (and hopefully used) the SMART (strategic and specific, measurable, attainable, results oriented, and time bound; Conzemius & O'Neill, 2014) acronym for goal development.

We won't go into much detail here about the SMART goal-setting process. Instead, following are some additional aspects of goal setting for you to consider in your trauma-sensitive implementation.

- **Written:** Written goals are visible and help ensure they are implemented.

- **Publicly shared:** Sharing goals outside of the school (within the community, with the parents, and so on) helps increase the commitment to them and their chances of success.

- **Small number:** If you select a small number of goals, you can concentrate on them and make them happen.

- **Collaboratively developed and shared:** Goals that include others' input and ideas improve their chances of success. In education, we call this *buy-in*. The success of your goals depends on collaboration and sharing.

- **A central part of the culture:** Goals that are a central part of the culture, posted, discussed regularly, and continuously refined are more likely to be accomplished than those written and filed away somewhere.

Principals can use a variety of strategies to get buy-in on the goals. Some might form a guiding coalition to discuss the issues and develop goals related to trauma-sensitive instruction, while others might engage their collaborative teams in this task. We have used building leadership teams to assist in developing and communicating goals. Whatever the means used to develop them, clear and specific goals are foundational to the success of your trauma-sensitive implementation.

Let's see how Principal Fountaine engages with her staff in following up and making sure they are implementing the strategies the leadership team developed for everyone to implement.

> About halfway through the implementation of the trauma-sensitive school project, Principal Fountaine starts to notice that some staff are not following up on the strategies they agreed to implement. Some have reverted to their old practices. More students are being sent to the office after having confrontations with the teachers. Principal Fountaine knows that it is time to gather data about their progress and consider making some midcourse corrections.
>
> For the next week, as she completes her walk-through visits, Principal Fountaine notes how often she sees teachers practicing and reinforcing the main calming strategies the staff agreed to implement. She shares the general information she gathered with

the building leadership team and engages them in identifying some techniques to get the trauma-sensitive implementation back on track. The leadership team decides to work with the school collaborative teams to remind teachers to review the strategies and work together to make sure they are doing similar strategies.

Within each of the school collaborative teams, teachers discuss the agreed-on strategies and then talk about how they initially worked and how they plan to launch them again. The teams discuss how they will review and implement each strategy, provide coaching and support for each other, and share ideas for how to improve it. After three weeks of support, most of the teachers are practicing the strategies with much success.

In this example, Principal Fountaine used her presence and encouragement to reinforce teachers to follow expectations. She used her positive comments and positional power as the principal to let everyone know they needed to be implementing the strategies. If she noticed that someone was not doing what was expected, she would quietly remind them. If after the reminder, they still weren't doing what was expected, she would provide a more direct reminder. If the direct reminder didn't get a teacher to act, she would need to become more forceful and mandate the change. By following up, Principal Fountaine moves the entire implementation forward.

Build Capacity Within Your Staff

As you continue to implement your trauma-sensitive plan, it will be important to also build the capacity of your staff. Initially, you may help them acquire the skills to implement some of your initial trauma-sensitive practices, but as they master these initial skills, you'll want to move to more advanced strategies.

Building staff capacity should include not only those who teach students, but everyone who has contact with students, such as bus drivers, custodians, food service staff, and others. An uninformed bus driver could trigger an incident by making an off-the-cuff comment if he or she doesn't know how to handle trauma-related situations.

You can build staff capacity through traditional means, such as attendance at professional development seminars, but also through a variety of alternative, job-embedded strategies such as the following.

- Book or topic study groups

- Drop-in short topic discussions before or after school

- Individual or team observations of teachers demonstrating trauma-sensitive practices (or they can watch videos)

- One-on-one sessions with instructional coaches

- Off-site professional development sessions

- Inclusion of trauma-sensitive practices in job descriptions and employee evaluation expectations

As the trauma-sensitive implementation continues, it's up to leaders to assess the progress of the entire staff, and then develop plans to bring everyone along so most of the staff are in agreement with the focus on trauma-sensitive change. This assessment could involve formal surveys, discussions in small groups or focus groups, informal conversations between the building leadership team and collaborative team members, or a variety of other assessment processes. By helping all staff gain the basic skills to be successful, you help ensure that trauma-impacted students experience consistency throughout their school day.

Plan Celebrations for Success

In the previous chapter, we discussed the importance of celebrations. Let's see how Principal Fountaine uses celebrations to motivate her staff.

> After about three months of implementing trauma-sensitive strategies, Principal Fountaine notices that most of the teachers are implementing several core trauma-sensitive strategies successfully. She provides reinforcement and coaching to each staff member after she visits their classrooms. She also shares ideas that teachers can use to improve how they implement the strategies. Word quickly spreads about her reinforcements and the refinement areas she shared with the teachers. In general, they like Principal Fountaine's hands-on approach.

> The implementation plan developed by the building leadership team included a celebration once the staff reached the milestone that everyone was implementing the major strategies. Principal Fountaine meets with the building leadership team to talk about successes and to plan the first celebration.

In the planning meeting, team members share lots of ideas for the celebration. The leadership team decides to hold a banana split party. Here's how the banana split party works.

1. *The team schedules a staff meeting.*

2. *On the day of the staff meeting, someone places a banana in each staff member's mailbox. Attached to the banana is a note that says, "Please decorate this banana in any manner that you choose. Bring it to the staff meeting."*

3. *At the meeting, the leader asks staff members to meet in small groups. Within each group, members share their decorated bananas and the rationale behind the decorations.*

4. *Once groups are finished sharing, Principal Fountaine asks group members to share the greatest hits (of decoration) from each group.*

5. *After members share their greatest hits, Principal Fountaine has one of the school cooks bring in a cart with several flavors of ice cream, toppings, bowls, spoons, and so on.*

6. *She congratulates the group for its progress in implementing trauma-sensitive practices, tells group members how proud she is of them, and encourages them to make a banana split to celebrate their success.*

7. *The staff enjoy the surprise and the fact that Principal Fountaine really appreciates their work.*

During any new implementation, celebrations are an important part of the process. Principal Fountaine knows this and plans for periodic celebrations as the trauma-sensitive school implementation begins. These celebrations let the staff know that their efforts are appreciated and noticed.

In *Starting a Movement*, authors Williams and Hierck (2015) discuss the importance of celebrations. They state:

> Build in early celebrations to recognize early wins. If this work represents a departure from current practice and has your school embarking on a new journey, celebrate each toehold that you gain. In every moment of celebration, articulate the alignment to your school's guiding mantra. This provides clarity in terms of both expectations and accomplishments. (Williams & Hierck, 2015, p. 155)

In Williams and Hierck's (2015) analysis, celebrations serve the function of showing the step-by-step progress you are making toward the total success of the project. Celebrations provide what you need to keep persevering through adversity to reach your long-term goals. Celebrations allow you temporarily to take a step back and take stock in your accomplishments. They help you gain a perspective about how far you have come in your journey to become a trauma-sensitive school. Without periodic celebrations, people can become discouraged and feel unappreciated. Celebrations are a necessary ingredient in the success of any implementation.

Williams and Hierck (2015) go on to discuss the crucial role that celebrations have in schools and in their growth. They state:

> Aligned celebration helps sustain the momentum for change, validates the initiators and movers, and convinces the holdouts that the work is worth the struggle. [Celebration] draws a staff together to acknowledge their own efforts and to enjoy time together in a less structured environment. (Williams & Hierck, 2015, p. 159)

Several key elements are outlined in this quote. First, the authors point out the concept of "aligned celebrations." That means celebrations are related to and support the change. In aligning celebrations, let staff know *why* you are celebrating. A second key point relates to the "holdouts" related to the change. When celebrating success, let the holdouts know you are serious and committed to the success of the change. Celebrations help institutionalize or legitimize the change.

In their best-selling book, *Energizing Staff Meetings*, Eller and Eller (2006) share some simple, yet effective ideas for celebrating small victories.

- **High five:** This is a simple, yet effective strategy. During a meeting, when an announcement is made that relates to a part of the success during an implementation, play energizing music as teachers come together into the center of the room to give each other a high five.

- **Banana split:** Teachers get a banana, decorate it, and use it to make a banana split at an after-school meeting (as previously described in the scenario for this section).

- **Rewards and rituals:** We know the power of rituals in trauma-sensitive classrooms. Rewards and rituals also provide motivation for staff implementing trauma-sensitive instruction. Starting staff meetings with good news or asking staff to share a productive strategy they recently used can build their mindset for success. Providing some form of award can also be motivating. You could fill small (unique) dishes with candy and then hold a drawing for those who submitted a trauma-sensitive success story. You can either announce the winners over the intercom or give out the rewards at a staff meeting.

- **Get-out-of-duty cards:** Staff members normally don't look forward to doing their extra duty (lunch supervision, recess supervision, bus supervision, and so on). Make up cards modeled after the *Monopoly* "Get Out of Jail" card, and you can issue them as prizes for sharing success stories related to trauma-sensitive successes. Staff can hold onto these cards and use them whenever they need them.

The ideas of things you can use for celebrations are only limited by your imagination. If you are using a building leadership team to guide implementation, they can help generate ideas for celebration. Sometimes, it can also be helpful to open up the brainstorming of celebration ideas to the entire staff. No matter how you decide on what to use in your celebrations, they help ensure that your staff get energized and motivated to continue their journey in becoming a trauma-sensitive school.

Figure 7.2 shows an example template for planning aligned celebrations.

I would like to recognize _____ for _____.
Your actions reflect a culture of collective responsibility because:

_____

_____

_____

_____

Given by: _____   Date: _____

Source: Adapted from Williams & Hierck, 2015.

Figure 7.2: Sample aligned celebration form.

Data Gathering and Analysis to Assess Trauma-Sensitive Practices

In order to track the implementation and identify potential areas that need adjustment, it's a good idea to formally assess your trauma-sensitive implementation journey. This could be done in a manner similar to how leaders and leadership teams assess academic improvement projects.

Let's see how Principal Fountaine implements assessment in the trauma-sensitive project at her school:

Toward the end of the year, the teachers at Dakota Elementary School are doing a good job of implementing the three agreed-on classroom stability and calming strategies. As Principal Fountaine completes her walk-through visits, she sees that things are going well. In talking with members of the staff, the collaborative teams, and the building leadership team, it seems like everything is going well.

Principal Fountaine decides to move beyond her assumptions and gather data related to the trauma-sensitive practices implementation. She knows that data would help her and everyone else see how things are actually going.

The leadership team has experience over the last ten years in gathering student achievement data, evaluating the results, and developing plans to address student needs. Principal Fountaine wants them to now make the move from strictly testing and academic assessments to data that may not be as clear and easy to gather. She works with them to first identify some of the indicators of success and then find a way to review and analyze these key indicators.

The leadership team identifies the following areas for data gathering and analysis:

- *Student office referrals*
- *Student absenteeism*
- *The results of a survey to be administered to teachers*
- *The results of a trauma-sensitive survey to be administered to students*
- *Teacher interviews and focus groups*

Team members will analyze the data and put it together to help them understand what happened during the implementation of trauma-sensitive practices in the school.

In this scenario, Principal Fountaine gathers some data to track how the trauma-sensitive strategies are working. In this case, she decides to focus on a few existing and available data sources. By keeping the data analysis simple and straightforward, she is able to help her staff get an indication of their progress. This straightforward focus is similar to taking someone's temperature or checking the oil in a car. For tracking ongoing implementations, an indication is usually enough.

In the implementations we have led, and in those we have supported, holding periodic, problem-solving meetings also has been helpful. For these problem-solving meetings to be helpful in assessing your implementation, they should include the following.

- A review of progress to date
- A review of the positive aspects of the implementation
- A review of the challenges or problems that have emerged as a result of the implementation
- A conversation or the development of a plan to address the challenges and keep the implementation on track
- Setting the date for the next problem-solving meeting

When conducting a problem-solving meeting with staff, it's a good idea to have a clear and easy-to-follow plan. Figure 7.3 provides a planning template you can use to conduct problem-solving meetings.

You can conduct these problem-solving meetings with the building leadership team, as a part of collaborative team meetings, or together with the entire staff at a large group meeting. Whether you talk in a large group or meet in smaller teams to discuss the implementation depends on what you think would be most productive for your specific situation and school.

A word of caution here. It's easy for these problem-solving meetings to become complaint sessions. While it's important to give people the opportunity to air their concerns, make sure they understand the importance of moving beyond complaints toward developing strategies to overcome the challenges and keep the trauma-sensitive implementation on track.

1. What are your outcomes or objectives for the meeting? How will you know if these objectives are met?

   _____

   _____

   _____

   _____

   _____

2. What are some issues that might get the meeting off track or distract the group from generating solutions to the issues? If these issues arise, how do you plan to address them so the group can move forward?

   _____

   _____

   _____

   _____

   _____

3. What process or processes do you plan to use to brainstorm ideas to address the concerns brought up by the group? Will you use verbal strategies, written ideas, or a combination of both?

   _____

   _____

   _____

   _____

   _____

4. What sort of timeline do you plan to implement in getting started with the strategies? How do you plan to measure your efforts and report them back to the larger group?

   _____

   _____

   _____

   _____

   _____

Figure 7.3: Problem-solving meeting planning template.

*Visit **go.SolutionTree.com/leadership** for a free reproducible version of this figure.*

Conclusion

Moving beyond the success of an initial or trial implementation can be difficult. Working toward long-range success takes planning and work. In this chapter, you learned strategies for planning and implementing trauma-sensitive practices for the second year and beyond. While each trauma-sensitive implementation is unique, we hope you gained ideas and strategies you can use to help make your implementation a success. While implementing trauma-sensitive practices can be challenging, it is also rewarding and good for all students' success.

QUESTIONS FOR *Reflection*

As you think about what you learned in this chapter and how it can be implemented in your school, reflect on the following questions.

- Why is it important to help staff manage the change process as they implement trauma-sensitive practices?

- What are some of the purposes of celebrations? How can celebrations help staff to see that the trauma-sensitive implementation is serious and will continue?

- Why are transitions in change so important? How can a school leader help staff to navigate these transitions?

References and Resources

Adams, J. M. (2013, December 2). *Schools promoting 'trauma-informed' teaching to reach troubled students.* Accessed at https://edsource.org/2013/schools-focus-on-trauma -informed-to-reach-troubled-students/51619 on February 2, 2022.

Alisic, E. (2012). Teachers' perspectives on providing support to children after trauma: A qualitative study. *School Psychology Quarterly, 27*(1), 51–59. Accessed at www.apa .org/pubs/journals/features/spq-27-1-51.pdf on December 17, 2020.

American Psychological Association. (2003). Guidelines on multicultural education, training, research, practice, and organizational change for psychologists. *American Psychologist, 58*(5), 377–402.

American Psychological Association. (2014a). *Parent engagement in schools.* Accessed at www.apa.org/pi/lgbt/programs/safe-supportive/parental-engagement/default.aspx on October 20, 2020.

American Psychological Association. (2014b). *The road to resilience.* Accessed at https://uncw.edu/studentaffairs/committees/pdc/documents/the%20road%20to %20resilience.pdf on October 20, 2020.

Arlinghaus, K. R., & Johnston, C. A. (2019). The importance of creating habits and routine. *American Journal of Lifestyle Medicine, 13*(2), 142–144.

Atkins, M.-A., & Rodger, S. (2016). Pre-service teacher education for mental health and inclusion in schools. *Exceptionality Education International, 26*(2), 93–118.

Blackboard. (2016). *Trends in community engagement: How K–12 schools are meeting the expectations of parents for digital communications.* Accessed at https://tomorrow.org /speakup/2016-digital-learning-reports-from-blackboard-and-speak-up.html on October 20, 2020.

BrainyQuote. (n.d.a). *John Kenneth Galbraith quotes.* (n.d.). Accessed at www.brainyquote .com/quotes/john_kenneth_galbraith_109909 on November 22, 2021.

BrainyQuote. (n.d.b). *Zig Ziglar quotes.* Accessed at www.brainyquote.com/quotes/zig _ziglar_381975 on November 9, 2021.

Bridges, W. (2016). *Managing transitions: Making the most of change* (4th ed.). Boston: Da Capo Lifelong Books.

Brunzell, T., Stokes, H., & Waters, L. (2016). Trauma-informed positive education: Using positive psychology to strengthen vulnerable students. *Contemporary School Psychology, 20*(1), 63–83.

Brunzell, T., Waters, L., & Stokes, H. (2015). Teaching with strengths in trauma-affected students: A new approach to healing and growth in the classroom. *American Journal of Orthopsychiatry, 85*(1), 3–9.

Centers for Disease Control and Prevention. (2012). *Parent engagement: Strategies for involving parents in school health.* Accessed at www.cdc.gov/healthyyouth/protective /pdf/parent_engagement_strategies.pdf on October 20, 2020.

Centers for Disease Control and Prevention. (2020a). *About the CDC-Kaiser ACE study.* Accessed at www.cdc.gov/violenceprevention/aces/about.html on October 20, 2020.

Centers for Disease Control and Prevention. (2020b). *Adverse childhood experiences (ACEs).* Accessed at www.cdc.gov/violenceprevention/acestudy on October 20, 2020.

Centers for Disease Control and Prevention. (2021). *Preventing adverse childhood experiences.* Accessed at www.cdc.gov/violenceprevention/aces/fastfact.html on August 16, 2021.

Cherry, K. (2020, September 18). *How does implicit bias influence behavior? Explanations and impacts of unconscious bias.* Accessed at www.verywellmind.com/implicit-bias -overview-4178401 on February 2, 2022.

Child Trends. (2018, September 16). *Parental involvement in schools.* Accessed at www .childtrends.org/?indicators=parental-involvement-in-schools on October 20, 2020.

Childhelp. (n.d.). *Child abuse statistics and facts.* Accessed at www.childhelp.org/child -abuse-statistics on June 28, 2021.

Cobb, F., & Krownapple, J. (2019). *Belonging through a culture of dignity: The keys to successful equity implementation.* San Diego, CA: Mimi & Todd Press.

Cole, S. F., Eisner, A., Gregory, M., & Ristuccia, J. (2013). *Helping traumatized children learn: Creating and advocating for trauma-sensitive schools.* Boston: Massachusetts Advocates for Children. Accessed at https://traumasensitiveschools.org/wp-content /uploads/2013/11/HTCL-Vol-2-Creating-and-Advocating-for-TSS.pdf on June 25, 2021.

Conzemius, A. E., & O'Neill, J. (2014). *The handbook for SMART school teams: Revitalizing best practices for collaboration* (2nd ed.). Bloomington, IN: Solution Tree Press.

Cook, A., Spinazzola, J., Ford, J., Lanktree, C., Blaustein, M., Cloitre, M., et al. (2005). Complex trauma in children and adolescents. *Psychiatric Annals, 35*(5), 390–398.

Covey, S. R. (2013). *The seven habits of highly effective people: Powerful lessons in personal change* (25th anniversary ed.). New York: Simon & Schuster.

Craig, S. E. (2016a). *Trauma-sensitive schools: Learning communities transforming children's lives, K–5.* New York: Teachers College Press.

Craig, S. E. (2016b). The trauma-sensitive teacher. *Educational Leadership, 74*(1), 28–32. Accessed at www.ascd.org/publications/educational_leadership/sept16/vol74/num01 /The_Trauma-Sensitive_Teacher.aspx on October 20, 2020.

Crecco, J. (2017, August). The adverse childhood experiences (ACE) study: A hidden public health crisis. *Federation for Children With Special Needs Newsletter*, 13–14. Accessed at https://fcsn.org/newsletter/2017/August on June 24, 2021.

Curby, T. W., Rudasill, K. M., Edwards, T., & Pérez-Edgar, K. (2011). The role of classroom quality in ameliorating the academic and social risks associated with difficult temperament. *School Psychology Quarterly*, *26*(2), 175–188.

Dearing, E., Kreider, H., Simpkins, S., & Weiss, H. B. (2006). Family involvement in school and low-income children's literacy: Longitudinal associations between and within families. *Journal of Educational Psychology*, *98*(4), 653–664.

Downey, L. (2007). *Calmer classrooms: A guide to working with traumatised children.* Melbourne, Victoria, Australia: Child Safety Commissioner. Accessed at www.paces connection.com/g/aces-in-education/fileSendAction/fcType/5/fcOid/45293488939 1655998/fodoid/452934889391655997/Calmer%20Classrooms%20-%20A%20guide %20to%20working%20with%20traumatised%20children.pdf on October 21, 2020.

Duckworth, A. (2016). *Grit: The power of passion and perseverance.* New York: Scribner.

Duke University. (2017, December 1). *Dropping out of high school linked to child abuse.* Accessed at www.sciencedaily.com/releases/2017/12/171201131636.htm on February 27, 2021.

Dweck, C. S. (2016). *Mindset: The new psychology of success* (Updated ed.). New York: Ballantine Books.

Dweck, C. S. (2017). The journey to children's mindsets—and beyond. *Child Development Perspectives*, *11*(2), 139–144.

Easterlin, M. C., Chung, P. J., Leng, M., & Dudovitz, R. (2019). Association of team sports participation with long-term mental health outcomes among individuals exposed to adverse childhood experiences. *JAMA Pediatrics*, *173*(7), 681–688. Accessed at https://pubmed.ncbi.nlm.nih.gov/31135890 on October 20, 2020.

Education Support. (2020). *Teacher wellbeing index 2020.* Accessed at www.education support.org.uk/sites/default/files/teacher_wellbeing_index_2020.pdf on February 27, 2021.

Egger, H. L., & Angold, A. (2006). Common emotional and behavioral disorders in preschool children: Presentation, nosology, and epidemiology. *Journal of Child Psychology and Psychiatry*, *47*(3–4), 313–337.

El Nokali, N. E., Bachman, H. J., & Votruba-Drzal, E. (2010). Parent involvement and children's academic and social development in elementary school. *Child Development*, *81*(3), 988–1005.

Eller, J. F., & Eller, S. A. (2009). *Creative strategies to transform school culture.* Thousand Oaks, CA: Corwin Press.

Eller, J. F., & Eller, S. A. (2011). *Working with difficult and resistant staff.* Bloomington, IN: Solution Tree Press.

Eller, J. F., & Eller, S. A. (2015). *Score to soar: Moving teachers from evaluation to professional growth*. Bloomington, IN: Solution Tree Press.

Eller, J. F., & Eller, S. A. (2016). *Thriving as a new teacher: Tools and strategies for your first year*. Bloomington, IN: Solution Tree Press.

Eller, J. F., & Eller, S. A. (2019). *Flip this school: How to lead the turnaround process*. Bloomington, IN: Solution Tree Press.

Eller, J. F., & Hierck, T. (2021). *Trauma-sensitive instruction: Creating a safe and predictable classroom environment*. Bloomington, IN: Solution Tree Press.

Eller, S. A., & Eller, J. F. (2006). *Energizing staff meetings*. Thousand Oaks, CA: Corwin Press.

Engagement. (n.d.). In *Merriam-Webster's online dictionary*. Accessed at www.merriam -webster.com/dictionary/engagement on February 3, 2021.

Felitti, V. J. (2019). Origins of the ACE study. *American Journal of Preventive Medicine, 56*(6), 787–789.

Felitti, V. J., & Anda, R. F. (2009). *The adverse childhood experiences (ACE) study: Bridging the gap between childhood trauma and negative consequences later in life*. Accessed at www.acestudy.org on April 12, 2021.

Felitti, V. J., & Anda, R. F. (2010). The relationship of adverse childhood experiences to adult medical disease, psychiatric disorders and sexual behavior: Implications for healthcare. In R. A. Lanius, E. Vermetten, & C. Pain (Eds.), *The impact of early life trauma on health and disease: The hidden epidemic* (pp. 77–87). New York: Cambridge University Press.

Felitti, V. J., Anda, R. F., Nordenberg, D., Williamson, D. F., Spitz, A. M., Edwards, V., et al. (1998). Relationship of childhood abuse and household dysfunction to many of the leading causes of death in adults: The Adverse Childhood Experiences (ACE) Study. *American Journal of Preventive Medicine, 14*(4), 245–258. Accessed at www .ajpmonline.org/article/S0749-3797(98)00017-8/fulltext on September 30, 2021.

Ferlazzo, L. (2011). Involvement or engagement? *Educational Leadership, 68*(8), 10–14. Accessed at www.ascd.org/publications/educational-leadership/may11/vol68/num08 /Involvement-or-Engagement%C2%A2.aspx on October 21, 2020.

Forbes, H. T. (2012). *Help for Billy: A beyond consequences approach to helping challenging children in the classroom*. Boulder, CO: Beyond Consequences Institute.

Ginott, H. G. (1972). *Teacher and child: A book for parents and teachers*. New York: Macmillan.

Glasser, W. (1999). *Choice theory: A new psychology of personal freedom*. New York: HarperPerennial.

Goodreads. (n.d.). *Theodore Roosevelt quotes*. Accessed at www.goodreads.com /quotes/34690-people-don-t-care-how-much-you-know-until-they-know on December 20, 2021.

Gough, P. B. (1991). Tapping parent power. *Phi Delta Kappan, 72*(5), 339.

Grand Rapids Public Schools. (n.d.). *Parent engagement: Partnering together*. Accessed at www.grps.org/parents/parental-engagement on February 27, 2021.

Guarino, K., & Chagnon, E. (2018). *Trauma-sensitive schools training package*. Washington, DC: National Center on Safe Supportive Learning Environments. Accessed at https://files.eric.ed.gov/fulltext/ED595276.pdf on June 25, 2021.

Hammond, Z. (2015). *Culturally responsive teaching and the brain: Promoting authentic engagement and rigor among culturally and linguistically diverse students*. Thousand Oaks, CA: Corwin Press.

Hawkins, J. D., Catalano, R. F., Kosterman, R., Abbott, R., & Hill, K. G. (1999). Preventing adolescent health-risk behaviors by strengthening protection during childhood. *Archives of Pediatrics and Adolescent Medicine, 153*(3), 226–234.

Henderson, A. T., & Berla, N. (Eds.). (1994). *A new generation of evidence: The family is critical to student achievement*. Washington, DC: National Committee for Citizens in Education.

Hierck, T. (2017). *Seven keys to a positive learning environment in your classroom*. Bloomington, IN: Solution Tree Press.

Hierck, T. (2019). *Managing unstoppable learning*. Bloomington, IN: Solution Tree Press.

Hill, N. E., & Tyson, D. F. (2009). Parental involvement in middle school: A meta-analytic assessment of the strategies that promote achievement. *Developmental Psychology, 45*(3), 740–763. Accessed at www.ncbi.nlm.nih.gov/pmc/articles/PMC2782391 on October 21, 2020.

Hobbs, C., Paulsen, D., & Thomas, J. (2019). *Trauma-informed practice for pre-service teachers*. Accessed at https://oxfordre.com/education/view/10.1093/acrefore/9780190264093.001.0001/acrefore-9780190264093-e-1435 on February 2, 2022.

Hord, S. M., Rutherford, W. L., Huling-Austin, L., & Hall, G. E. (1987). *Taking charge of change*. Alexandria, VA: Association for Supervision and Curriculum Development.

Hulley, W., & Dier, L. (2005). *Harbors of hope: The planning for school and student success process*. Bloomington, IN: National Educational Service.

Involvement. (n.d.). In *Merriam-Webster's online dictionary*. Accessed at www.merriam-webster.com/dictionary/involvement on February 3, 2021.

Jensen, E. (2013). *Engaging students with poverty in mind: Practical strategies for raising achievement*. Alexandria, VA: Association for Supervision and Curriculum Development.

Jensen, E., & McConchie, L. (2020). *Brain-based learning: Teaching the way students really learn* (3rd ed.). Thousand Oaks, CA: Corwin Press.

Kagan, J., & Segal, J. (1988). *Psychology: An introduction* (6th ed.). San Diego, CA: Harcourt Brace Jovanovich.

Kidder, R. M. (2006). *Moral courage*. New York: Harper.

Kidder, T. (2001). *Among schoolchildren*. New York: Perennial.

Kohn, A. (2005). Unconditional teaching. *Educational Leadership, 63*(1), 20–24. Accessed at www.ascd.org/ASCD/pdf/journals/ed_lead/el200509_kohn.pdf on October 21, 2020.

Kotter, J. (2012). *Leading change.* Boston: Harvard Business Review Press.

Kouzes, J. M., & Posner, B. Z. (2017). *The leadership challenge: How to make extraordinary things happen in organizations* (6th ed.). Hoboken, NJ: Wiley.

Logan, D., King, J., & Fischer-Wright, H. (2008). *Tribal leadership: Leveraging natural groups to build a thriving organization.* New York: Collins.

Lu, W. (2017). Child and adolescent mental disorders and health care disparities: Results from the National Survey of Children's Health, 2011–2012. *Journal of Health Care for the Poor and Underserved, 28*(3), 988–1011.

Makri-Botsari, E. (2001). Causal links between academic intrinsic motivation, self-esteem, and unconditional acceptance by teachers in high school students. In R. J. Riding & S. G. Rayner (Eds.), *International perspectives on individual differences: Self perception* (Vol. 2, pp. 209–220). Westport, CT: Ablex.

Marzano, R. J. (2017). *The new art and science of teaching.* Bloomington, IN: Solution Tree Press.

McInerney, M., & McKlindon, A. (2014). *Unlocking the door to learning: Trauma-informed classrooms and transformational schools.* Philadelphia: Education Law Center. Accessed at www.elc-pa.org/wp-content/uploads/2015/06/Trauma-Informed-in-Schools-Classrooms-FINAL-December2014-2.pdf on December 15, 2020.

Merrick, M. T., Ford, D. C., Ports, K. A., Guinn, A. S., Chen, J., Klevens, J., et al. (2019). Vital signs: Estimated proportion of adult health problems attributable to adverse childhood experiences and implications for prevention—25 States, 2015–2017. *Morbidity and Mortality Weekly Report, 68*(44), 999–1005. Accessed at www.cdc.gov/mmwr/volumes/68/wr/mm6844e1.htm?s_cid=mm6844e1_w on August 16, 2021.

Michigan Department of Education. (2015). *"Collaborating for success" parent engagement toolkit.* Accessed at www.michigan.gov/documents/mde/4a._Final_Toolkit_without_bookmarks_370151_7.pdf on January 22, 2021.

Mullainathan, S., & Shafir, E. (2013). *Scarcity: The new science of having less and how it defines our lives.* New York: Picador.

National Association of School Psychologists School Safety and Crisis Response Committee. (2015). *Supporting students experiencing childhood trauma: Tips for parents and educators.* Accessed at www.nasponline.org/resources-and-publications/resources-and-podcasts/school-climate-safety-and-crisis/mental-health-resources/trauma/supporting-students-experiencing-childhood-trauma-tips-for-parents-and-educators on March 2, 2021.

National Center for Education Statistics. (2018). *Fast facts: Back to school statistics.* Accessed at https://nces.ed.gov/fastfacts/display.asp?id=372 on December 15, 2020.

National Center for Mental Health Promotion and Youth Violence Prevention. (2012). *Childhood trauma and its effects on healthy development.* Accessed at www.ccpa.net /DocumentCenter/View/21000 on August 18, 2021.

National Child Traumatic Stress Network. (n.d.). *Families and trauma.* Accessed at www .nctsn.org/trauma-informed-care/families-and-trauma#page on October 13, 2021.

National Child Traumatic Stress Network. (2011, February). *Trauma and families: Fact sheet for providers.* Accessed at www.nctsn.org/sites/default/files/resources//trauma _and_families_providers.pdf on June 28, 2021.

National Child Traumatic Stress Network. (2017a). *Addressing race and trauma in the classroom: A resource for educators.* Accessed at www.nctsn.org/sites/default/files /resources//addressing_race_and_trauma_in_the_classroom_educators.pdf on June 28, 2021.

National Child Traumatic Stress Network. (2017b). *Family engagement and involvement in trauma mental health.* Accessed at www.nctsn.org/sites/default/files/resources/fact -sheet/cac_family_engagement_and_involvement_in_trauma_mental_health.pdf on February 28, 2021.

National Council of State Education Associations. (2019, July). *Addressing the epidemic of trauma in schools.* Washington, DC: National Education Association. Accessed at www.nea.org/sites/default/files/2020-09/Addressing%20the%20Epidemic%20of% 20Trauma%20in%20Schools%20-%20NCSEA%20and%20NEA%20Report.pdf on June 24, 2021.

National Parent Teacher Association. (2000). *Building successful partnerships: A guide for developing parent and family involvement programs.* Bloomington, IN: National Educational Service.

National Scientific Council on the Developing Child. (2015). *Supportive relationships and active skill-building strengthen the foundations of resilience.* Cambridge, MA: Center on the Developing Child, Harvard University. Accessed at https://developingchild .harvard.edu/wp-content/uploads/2015/05/The-Science-of-Resilience.pdf on October 21, 2020.

Nealy-Oparah, S., & Scruggs-Hussein, T. C. (2018). Trauma-informed leadership in schools: From the inside-out. *Leadership, 47*(3), 12–16.

Oehlberg, B. (2012). *Ending the shame: Transforming public education so it works for all students.* Pittsburgh, PA: RoseDog Books.

Organisation for Economic Co-operation and Development. (2021). *Parental involvement.* Accessed at https://gpseducation.oecd.org/revieweducationpolicies/#!node=41727 &filter=all on June 28, 2021.

Park, D., Tsukayama, E., Yu, A., & Duckworth, A. (2020). The development of grit and growth mindset during adolescence. *Journal of Experimental Child Psychology, 198*, 104889.

Perry, B. (n.d.). *The three R's: Reaching the learning brain.* Accessed at https://beaconhouse .org.uk/wp-content/uploads/2019/09/The-Three-Rs.pdf on December 20, 2021.

Perry, B. D. (2016, December 13). *The brain science behind student trauma.* Accessed at www.edweek.org/ew/articles/2016/12/14/the-brain-science-behind-student-trauma .html on October 21, 2020.

Rice, K. F., & Groves, B. M. (2005). *Hope and healing: A caregiver's guide to helping young children affected by trauma.* Washington, DC: Zero to Three Press.

Richardson, V. (1996). The role of attitudes and beliefs in learning to teach. In J. Sikula (Ed.), *Handbook of research on teacher education* (2nd ed., pp. 102–119). New York: Macmillan.

Robbins, A. (1986). *Unlimited power: The new science of personal achievement.* New York: Simon and Schuster.

Roberts, M. (2019). *Enriching the learning: Meaningful extensions for proficient students in a PLC at Work.* Bloomington, IN: Solution Tree Press.

Rogers, C. R. (1961). *On becoming a person: A therapist's view of psychotherapy.* Boston: Houghton Mifflin.

Schein, E. H. (2017). *Organizational culture and leadership* (5th ed.). Hoboken, NJ: Wiley.

Schickedanz, A., Halfon, N., Sastry, N., & Chung, P. J. (2018). Parents' adverse childhood experiences and their children's behavioral health problems. *Pediatrics, 142*(2). Accessed at https://pediatrics.aappublications.org/content/142/2/e20180023 on October 21, 2020.

Schwartz, H. L., Grant, D., Diliberti, M., Hunter, G. P., & Setodji, C. M. (2020). *Remote learning is here to stay: Results from the first American School District Panel survey.* Santa Monica, CA: RAND Corporation. Accessed at www.rand.org/pubs/research_reports /RRA956-1.html on February 28, 2021.

Sheldon, S. B., & Epstein, J. L. (2004). Getting students to school: Using family and community involvement to reduce chronic absenteeism. *School Community Journal, 14*(2), 39–56.

Sheldon, S. B., & Jung, S. B. (2015). *The family engagement partnership: Student outcome evaluation.* Baltimore: Johns Hopkins University. Accessed at www.pthvp.org/wp -content/uploads/2016/09/JHU-STUDY_FINAL-REPORT.pdf on October 21, 2020.

Skinner, B. F. (1953). *Science and human behavior.* New York: Free Press.

Smith, D., Frey, N., Pumpian, I., & Fisher, D. (2017). *Building equity: Policies and practices to empower all learners.* Alexandria, VA: Association for Supervision and Curriculum Development.

Smith, M., Robinson, L., & Segal, J. (2021). *Helping children cope with traumatic events.* Accessed at https://helpguide.org/articles/ptsd-trauma/helping-children-cope-with -traumatic-stress.htm on February 7, 2022.

Smith, R., Brofft, K., Law, N., & Smith, J. (2013). *The reflective leader: Implementing a multidimensional leadership performance system.* Englewood, CO: Lead + Learn Press.

Souers, K., & Hall, P. (2016). *Fostering resilient learners: Strategies for creating a trauma-sensitive classroom*. Alexandria, VA: Association for Supervision and Curriculum Development.

Souers, K., & Hall, P. (2019). *Relationship, responsibility, and regulation: Trauma-invested practices for fostering resilient learners*. Alexandria, VA: Association for Supervision and Curriculum Development.

Souers, K., & Hall, P. (2020). Trauma is a word—not a sentence. *Educational Leadership*, *78*(2), 34–39.

Sporleder, J., & Forbes, H. T. (2016). *The trauma-informed school: A step-by-step implementation guide for administrators and school personnel*. Boulder, CO: Beyond Consequences Institute.

Stafford, T., & Duchak, T. (2020). *Trauma in schools: A toolkit for educators and school administrators implementing trauma supports in schools*. Accessed at https://static1.squarespace.com/static/5871061e6b8f5b2a8ede8ff5/t/5f5014e19f357a52b866f8ba/1599083748081/Trauma+Toolkit+Final+FINAL.pdf on June 24, 2021.

Stamm, B. H., & Friedman, M. J. (2000). Cultural diversity in the appraisal and expression of trauma. In A. Y. Shalev, R. Yehuda, & A. C. McFarlane (Eds.), *International handbook of human response to trauma* (pp. 69–85). New York: Kluwer Academic.

Substance Abuse and Mental Health Services Administration. (2014). *SAMHSA's concept of trauma and guidance for a trauma-informed approach*. Accessed at https://ncsacw.samhsa.gov/userfiles/files/SAMHSA_Trauma.pdf on December 20, 2021.

Teicher, M. H., Andersen, S. L., Polcari, A., Anderson, C. M., Navalta, C. P., & Kim, D. M. (2003). The neurobiological consequences of early stress and childhood maltreatment. *Neuroscience and Biobehavioral Reviews*, *27*(1–2), 33–44.

Terrasi, S., & de Galarce, P. C. (2017). Trauma and learning in America's classrooms. *Phi Delta Kappan*, *98*(6), 35–41. Accessed at https://kappanonline.org/trauma-classrooms-learning on June 25, 2021.

Thomas, M. S., Crosby, S., & Vanderhaar, J. (2019). Trauma-informed practices in schools across two decades: An interdisciplinary review of research. *Review of Research in Education*, *43*(1), 422–452.

Tobin, M. (2016). *Childhood trauma: Developmental pathways and implications for the classroom*. Camberwell, Victoria, Australia: Australian Council for Educational Research. Accessed at https://research.acer.edu.au/learning_processes/20 on June 24, 2021.

Treatment and Services Adaptation Center. (n.d.). *Secondary traumatic stress*. Accessed at http://traumaawareschools.org/secondaryStress on December 12, 2020.

Tremblay, R. E. (1999). When children's social development fails. In D. P. Keating & C. Hertzman (Eds.), *Developmental health and the wealth of nations: Social, biological, and educational dynamics* (pp. 55–71). New York: Guilford Press.

Van Tieu, H., & Koblin, B. A. (2009). HIV, alcohol, and noninjection drug use. *Current Opinion in HIV and AIDS, 4*(4), 314–318.

Vogel, J. M., & Family Systems Collaborative Group. (2017). *Family resilience and traumatic stress: A guide for mental health providers.* Los Angeles: National Center for Child Traumatic Stress. Accessed at www.nctsn.org/sites/default/files/resources //family_resilience_and_traumatic_stress_providers.pdf on June 25, 2021.

Wairimu, M. J., Macharia, S. M., & Muiru, A. (2016). Analysis of parental involvement and self-esteem on secondary school students in Kieni West Sub-County, Nyeri County, Kenya. *Journal of Education and Practice, 7*(27), 82–98. Accessed at https:// files.eric.ed.gov/fulltext/EJ1115884.pdf on October 21, 2020.

Waterford.org. (2018, November 1). *How parent involvement leads to student success.* Accessed at www.waterford.org/education/how-parent-involvment-leads-to-student -success on December 15, 2020.

Watson, M. (2019). *Learning to trust: Attachment theory and classroom management* (2nd ed.). New York: Oxford University Press.

Weber, C. (2018). *Behavior: The forgotten curriculum—An RTI approach for nurturing essential life skills.* Bloomington, IN: Solution Tree Press.

WebMD. (2007). *TV violence—A cause of child anxiety and aggressive behavior?* Accessed at www.webmd.com/parenting/features/tv-violence-cause-child-anxiety-aggressive -behavior#1 on October 20, 2020.

Wilgoren, J. (2000, March 14). Florida's vouchers a spur to 2 schools left behind. *The New York Times.* Accessed at www.nytimes.com/2000/03/14/us/florida-s-vouchers-a-spur -to-2-schools-left-behind.html on October 21, 2020.

Williams, K. C., & Hierck, T. (2015). *Starting a movement: Building culture from the inside out in professional learning communities.* Bloomington, IN: Solution Tree Press.

Wolcott, G. (2019). *Significant 72: Unleashing the power of relationships in today's schools.* Oshkosh, WI: FIRST Educational Resources.

Wong, J. (2020, October 28). *Teachers say return to school this fall has left them with overwhelming stress and a never-ending workload.* Accessed at www.cbc.ca/news /canada/teacher-questionnaire-pandemic-1.5775805 on February 27, 2021.

Zenger, J., & Folkman, J. (2013, March 15). The ideal praise-to-criticism ratio. *Harvard Business Review.* Accessed at https://hbr.org/2013/03/the-ideal-praise-to-criticism on February 23, 2021.

Index

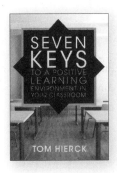

Seven Keys to a Positive Learning Environment in Your Classroom
Tom Hierck

Creating a positive classroom learning environment is a complex but necessary task. By following the seven keys the author outlines, teachers can establish clearer expectations, enhance instruction and assessment practices, and foster quality relationships with students, maximizing the potential of all students.

BKF721

Uniting Academic and Behavior Interventions
Austin Buffum, Mike Mattos, Chris Weber, and Tom Hierck

Ensure students acquire the academic skills, dispositions, and knowledge necessary for long-term success. Examine what effective academic and behavior supports look like for all learners. Explore a step-by-step process for determining, targeting, and observing academic and behavior interventions.

BKF595

Flip This School:
John F. Eller and Sheila A. Eller

Designed for administrators and teacher leaders, Flip This School presents a framework to lead a successful, sustainable school turnaround. Readers will gain a variety of practical strategies for planning school improvement efforts and collaborating with the existing staff to initiate a schoolwide transformation.

BKF669

Trauma-Sensitive Instruction
John F. Eller and Tom Hierck

Confidently and meaningfully support your trauma-impacted students with this accessible resource. The authors draw from their personal and professional experiences with trauma, mental health, and school culture to provide real insight into what you can do now to help learners build resilience and achieve at high levels.

BKF847

Wait! Your professional development journey doesn't have to end with the last pages of this book.

We realize improving student learning doesn't happen overnight. And your school or district shouldn't be left to puzzle out all the details of this process alone.

No matter where you are on the journey, we're committed to helping you get to the next stage.

Take advantage of everything from **custom workshops** to **keynote presentations** and **interactive web and video conferencing**. We can even help you develop an action plan tailored to fit your specific needs.

Let's get the conversation started.

Call 888.763.9045 today.

SolutionTree.com